Learning MIT
App Inventor

Addison-Wesley Learning Series

✦ Addison-Wesley

Visit informit.com/learningseries for a complete list of available publications.

The Addison-Wesley Learning Series is a collection of hands-on programming guides that help you quickly learn a new technology or language so you can apply what you've learned right away.

Each title comes with sample code for the application or applications built in the text. This code is fully annotated and can be reused in your own projects with no strings attached. Many chapters end with a series of exercises to encourage you to reexamine what you have just learned, and to tweak or adjust the code as a way of learning.

Titles in this series take a simple approach: they get you going right away and leave you with the ability to walk off and build your own application and apply the language or technology to whatever you are working on.

✦ Addison-Wesley   **informIT** | Safari
                    the trusted technology learning source   Books Online

Learning MIT App Inventor

A Hands-On Guide to Building Your Own Android Apps

Derek Walter
Mark Sherman

♠Addison-Wesley

Upper Saddle River, NJ • Boston • Indianapolis • San Francisco
New York • Toronto • Montreal • London • Munich • Paris • Madrid
Cape Town • Sydney • Tokyo • Singapore • Mexico City

For information about buying this title in bulk quantities, or for special sales opportunities (which may include electronic versions; custom cover designs; and content particular to your business, training goals, marketing focus, or branding interests), please contact our corporate sales department at corpsales@pearsoned.com or (800) 382-3419.

For government sales inquiries, please contact governmentsales@pearsoned.com.

For questions about sales outside the U.S., please contact international@pearsoned.com.

Visit us on the Web: informit.com/aw

Library of Congress Control Number: 2014950962

ISBN-13: 978-0-133-79863-0
ISBN-10: 0-133-79863-1

Text printed in the United States on recycled paper at RR Donnelley in Crawfordsville, Indiana.

First printing: December 2014

Editor-in-Chief
Mark Taub

Executive Editor
Laura Lewin

Senior Development Editor
Chris Zahn

Managing Editor
Kristy Hart

Project Editor
Elaine Wiley

Copy Editor
Krista Hansing
Editorial Services, Inc.

Indexer
Lisa Stumpf

Proofreader
Debbie Williams

Technical Reviewers
Tom Stokke
Arta Szathma
Janet Brown-Sederberg

Editorial Assistant
Olivia Basegio

Cover Designer
Chuti Prasertsith

Compositor
Nonie Ratcliff

❖

from Derek

This book is dedicated to my incredible wife, Candy.

from Mark

This book is dedicated to Stacy (depending on what she says).

❖

Table of Contents

Acknowledgments

from Derek

I want to thank my amazing wife, Candy, who supported me during the crucible of writing a book. Your strength and encouragement kept me going through the late nights, exhausting weekends, and challenges that came with this project.

I would like to thank the MIT App Inventor team members for their support and for continuing such an important project that is democratizing computer programming. Also, thank you to Laura Lewin and the Pearson team for their guidance with this first-time author.

from Mark

I want to thank the AI team at MIT, the AI Master Trainers program organizers, Lyn Turbak, and especially Fred Martin. All of you helped me get to this point, and all of this accrued knowledge is thanks to you.

I want to thank my close friends, all of whom endured my writing and working through many events, and often were kind enough to pull the laptop off my sleeping face. I appreciate it. I especially want to thank Stacy for taking care of me every step of the way. Stacy, will you marry me?

About the Authors

Derek Walter is a freelance writer specializing in the mobile ecosystem. He contributes regularly to PCWorld, Macworld, Greenbot, and other sites devoted to consumer technology. He also blogs about mobile apps and other topics in technology at theappplanet.com. His undergraduate degree is in mass communication/journalism, and he holds a master's degree in educational technology from The George Washington University. Derek has also worked in education for the last 15 years as a classroom teacher and adjunct university instructor.

Mark Sherman is a researcher in computer science education and has taught computing, programming, and robotics to undergraduates in the U.S., India, and China. He is an MIT App Inventor Master Trainer, and he has taught students mobile app design with App Inventor and trained teachers and faculty on best practices and pedagogy of the same. He holds a bachelor's degree in computer engineering and a master's degree in computer science, both from UMass Lowell.

Preface

The smartphone is the ultimate personal computer. Mobile devices are always with us and have become an essential part of personal productivity and lifestyle needs. We use them for messaging, social media, Google searches, games, picture taking, and, of course, phone calls.

The Android operating system powers most of the world's smartphones, bringing an extensive app catalog to these devices. According to Google, more than 1 billion active devices are currently running Android.

Perhaps you have reached the point at which using mobile apps on your smartphone isn't enough—it is time to create one. You might just want to tinker and program a simple app, or maybe you have thought of a new concept that doesn't exist yet. Whatever the case, MIT App Inventor is an excellent place to start.

App Inventor is an easy-to-use tool for building both simple and complex Android applications. The apps can easily be ported to your phone, shared with others, or even sent to the Google Play Store for distribution to all Android devices worldwide.

For those looking to learn a programming language, MIT App Inventor can serve as an excellent bridge to acquiring more complex coding skills. Instead of presenting new users with frustrating messages and unfamiliar commands, App Inventor has a visually friendly interface that uses the methods of dragging, dropping, and connecting puzzle pieces to program applications (see Figure P.1).

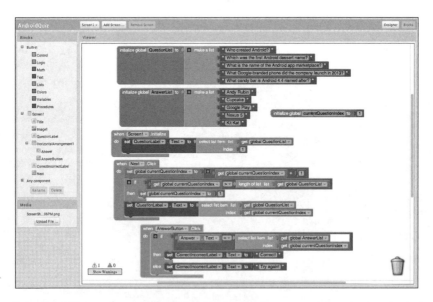

Figure P.1   The MIT App Inventor Blocks Editor. The visual programming is designed to help beginners learn the ropes of building mobile applications.

Even though App Inventor does not require using code, it builds on the same kinds of principles that successful programmers need to write good applications. Whether you go no further with programming or you use App Inventor to launch a new career, using App Inventor can be a highly engaging and challenging experience. Additionally, the open and flexible nature of Android makes it the perfect place to start.

What Is MIT App Inventor?

MIT App Inventor is a web-based tool for building Android apps (see Figure P.2). This is often referred to as visual programming, which means the user is able to perform programming tasks without entering any computer code.

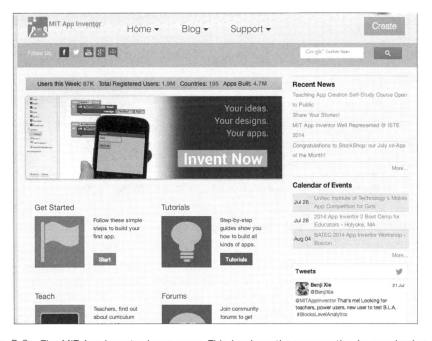

Figure P.2   The MIT App Inventor home page. This is where the app-creation journey begins.

App Inventor is actively managed and developed by MIT's Mobile Learning Lab (the project was originally built by Google). App Inventor is growing in popularity among educators as a way to introduce those with no programming experience to the principles of computer science and app development. It also serves as a great first step for those dabbling with programming or looking to increase their knowledge of how smartphone apps work.

The work takes place in two key sections of App Inventor: the Designer and the Blocks Editor. In the Designer, you decide what actions the app will perform and how it will look (see Figure P.3).

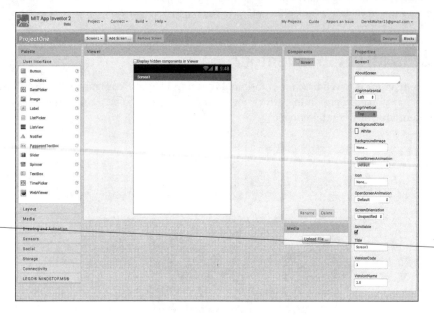

Figure P.3   In the App Inventor Designer, you design the app and add its key functionality.

The programming takes place in the Blocks Editor. There you tell the app what it should do and give specific instructions for making that happen.

The specific capabilities are programmed through connecting puzzle pieces. Over time, you will learn what each block does and find multiple ways for them to interact with one another. The pieces that do not interact will not connect with each other—another helpful way for beginners to get a sense of introductory programming principles.

MIT released App Inventor 2 in December 2013, creating a more powerful and easier-to-use tool. The most significant improvement is that all the work takes place within the browser (the previous version required a software download for some of the capabilities).

This improvement most impacts the onscreen emulator, which places a virtual Android device screen on your computer. Using this emulator provides a perspective on how the app will look and function when put to use. This is especially useful for those without an Android device or anyone in an education setting who wants to monitor student progress by viewing app builds on computer screens.

App Inventor also offers a method for using the app in real time while performing work on it: the AI Companion app (see Figure P.4). With this free download from Google Play, you can see your app change and develop while working on it. The Companion app also works wirelessly, so you don't need to physically connect your phone to a computer while working in App Inventor.

Figure P.4   An App Inventor app as viewed through the AI2 Companion. This lets you see both how the app is performing and how it looks while it is still being developed.

Why Android?

Android is not only the most popular operating system—it also is the most extendable. It is found on a wide variety of flagship devices from major handset makers, such as Samsung, HTC, LG, and Motorola. App Inventor is built to take advantage of the customization and flexibility that Android offers.

App Inventor is also a tool that is designed with those who have little to no programming experience in mind. Other platforms have a fairly high barrier of entry, but with App Inventor, you can more easily learn the essential skills for building an app with the world's most popular mobile platform.

Although many apps you create are likely to be used for practice or to share with others (see Figure P.5), MIT App Inventor is capable of creating apps that can be uploaded for distribution in the Google Play Store. With only a one-time fee of $25, anyone can put his or her skill set to work and become a registered Android developer. Chapter 12, "Distributing an App," discusses this process and walks through how to accomplish it.

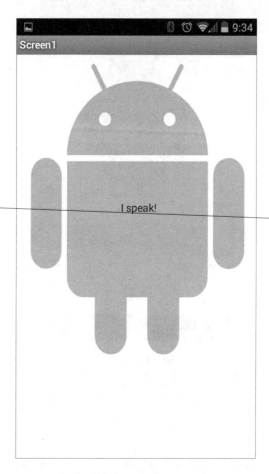

Figure P.5   An App Inventor app in the AI2 Companion.

What This Book Covers

So what exactly does this book discuss? The following sections provide a preview of the key highlights from the upcoming 12 chapters.

Chapter 1: An Introduction to Programming

Before getting started with MIT App Inventor, it is important to get some background in key computer science principles. This chapter addresses the key parts of a mobile operating system and how computer programmers should think about creating applications.

Chapter 2: Building with MIT App Inventor

This chapter provides the first detailed walkthrough of the key pieces of App Inventor. The Blocks Editor and Designer get fuller attention here, and you get to build your first app: Sherlock Is Watching.

Chapter 3: App Inventor Toolkit

App Inventor has some powerful yet easy-to-use tools for designing and building Android apps. In this chapter, the focus is on the different components available in the Designer. This serves as a good resource on the different capabilities of the Designer and will be a chapter worth referencing often.

Chapter 4: Variables

Variables are one of the key pieces of App Inventor; almost any app that you build will use them in some way. Chapter 4 covers the essentials of variables and provides some strategies for their effective use, particularly in the context of building the sample app for the chapter.

Chapter 5: Procedures

With some basic app building under your belt, it is time to take the next step and use procedures. Procedures make your life easier when it comes to building larger, more complicated apps because they enable you to group pieces of code together and recall it later.

Chapter 6: Working with Lists

As with variables, lists are a core piece of most apps that you will build with App Inventor. Lists store large pieces of data or information. The chapter culminates with a quiz app that provides some good practice in using lists.

Chapter 7: Games and Animations

Work and productivity alone are no fun. This chapter teaches the basics of the gaming and animation capabilities of App Inventor. It concludes with a simple game that could be a springboard for you to use App Inventor for other basic or more complex games.

Chapter 8: Multiple Screens and Debugging Techniques

Apps typically have multiple screens, giving users greater clarity and more streamlined access to the content of an app. This chapter focuses on strategies for using multiple screens and explores how to build them into applications. It also covers some debugging techniques for App Inventor.

Chapter 9: Using Media

Most of the smartphone apps that people use are media rich. Here you get some exposure to and practice in building media capabilities into your own apps, and you learn what is possible in App Inventor.

Chapter 10: Sensors

Many apps are location aware, letting users find specific information or customize their interaction based on location. This chapter shows you how to build some of these tools into your own apps and illustrates how they can improve a user's experience.

Chapter 11: Databases

Databases might not sound exciting, but they are a core feature of any good app that relies on storing information. This chapter looks at how to use databases effectively in different scenarios.

Chapter 12: Distributing an App

Keeping an app that you have built all to yourself is no fun. It is time to share it with others. This can be as simple as sending the file to friends and family or placing it in the Google Play Store for worldwide distribution. Whichever path you choose, this chapter assists you in getting to your destination.

Next Steps

Using App Inventor is an excellent way to build an Android app (see Figure P.6). As with many other skills in computer science, building a mobile application is an exercise in both creativity and logical thinking. You need to solve rational, complex problems while simultaneously building out a creative vision. Although you can learn App Inventor's basics rather quickly, you can build more powerful and complex applications with additional time and practice.

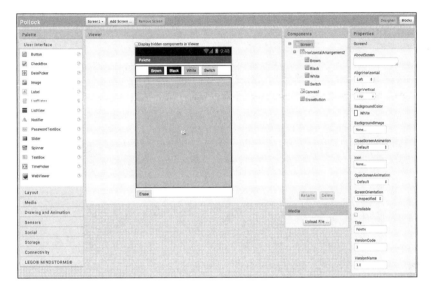

Figure P.6   You can create a variety of application types with App Inventor.

Chapter 1 begins with some essential computer science principles. Understanding how an operating system functions and what developers are actually doing when building software will give you a solid foundation in effective programming. With this established, you will be ready to build a variety of sample Android apps as you follow along in the book and then extend this skill set to your own Android apps.

An Introduction to Programming

In its most basic form, programming is telling a computer what to do. Modern programmers are increasingly focusing their efforts on building applications for the pocket computers we all carry: smartphones. Mobile apps have exploded in popularity because of the proliferation of mobile devices.

Understanding the programming process sets the foundation for the kind of thinking required to build excellent Android apps with MIT App Inventor. Even though you will not be using text-based programming with App Inventor, you will need to use the same kind of logical thinking, problem solving, and creativity that professional application developers use when writing programs.

Creating an app involves writing computer code. Yet learning a programming language is an involved process that is typically reserved for those who plan to become professional programmers. The strength of MIT App Inventor is that visual blocks are the code. You can build Android apps and program their functions by piecing together puzzle pieces and using drag-and-drop tools.

However, do not misconstrue this as a "minor league" or inferior version of programming. Creating programs in App Inventor requires the same kind of logical thinking, reasoning, and creativity as in traditional programming. Learning to think in this manner and knowing what is going on behind the scenes of what you see on a smartphone will make you more effective at creating great applications. It will also give you an excellent foundation if you plan to deepen your study of computer science and master one or more other programming languages.

Computational thinking requires a distinct set of meta-cognitive skills. Good programming involves being able to create logical, step-by-step commands that a computer or application will follow. Piecing together instructions and giving applications the capability to handle multiple pieces of data and events is what helps users know that they are working with a truly intelligent machine.

Operating Systems

To build strong applications, it is helpful to have at least a general knowledge of the operating system (OS) for which you are building. Over time, this will make you a better programmer and enhance your ability to build great applications. Although our focus in this text is Google's mobile operating system, Android, we first consider the general parts that make any operating system function.

In short, the operating system is the software that powers a computing device. It handles all the core functions, such as executing applications, running tasks, and controlling any peripherals.

Today's smartphones are computers—they carry all the characteristics and components of what once required a larger piece of machinery. They have a constant network connection and are capable of bringing in all types of data when requested by a program, such as using your location from the GPS sensor to determine the tilt of the phone. An operating system consists of several individual processes. A helpful way to visualize this is to see each of these processes as layers in a larger hierarchical structure.

At the lowest level of the OS is a kernel, which provides the most basic control over a device's hardware. It manages the memory access and determines which programs get to access the various hardware resources, such as the dialer or the camera.

Even if this is new information, you can start to see how the Android operating system provides an interface between the device and your app. This is important because it allows your app to work on a variety of devices. You, the programmer, just need to write an app that works with the Android operating system, freeing you from having to worry or deal with the intricacies of the diverse hardware options available (see Figure 1.1).

A series of libraries and application frameworks constitutes the next layer in the operating system, which is responsible for managing various data sets. The operating system creates an interface between applications and the device's hardware, ensuring effective information sharing and memory management (see Figure 1.2). Although it need not be a concern at this point, learning how an operating system manages its memory resources eventually will be important.

A significant factor in how well an operating system performs is its memory management. All devices have a limited amount of memory that must be allocated among the various resources, such as key operating system functions and applications. When performing more advanced programming, ensuring that your app is not using an excessive amount of memory will be a key component.

Figure 1.1   The Android settings display key operating system information, such as the version of Android.

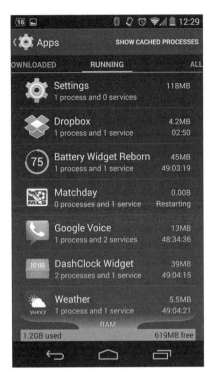

Figure 1.2   An operating system manages the background processes run by various applications. Android enables you to monitor and even take action to preserve system resources.

Programs have traditionally operated in a linear fashion, performing only one action at a time. When the program requested a piece of information from the user, the entire program stopped until that information was entered, and then the program continued. However, today's programs multitask. While using a smartphone, a user might be looking up directions on a map, for example. The device then is accessing a location via GPS, pulling in map data, and performing various other background tasks, such as pushing email or receiving instant notifications (see Figure 1.3).

Figure 1.3   Google Maps uses location for context when mapping an area.

As such, modern programming involves maximizing the use of such connected devices and smartly allocating smartphone resources. Mobile devices are constantly accessing data from multiple sources, which can make an app more interactive. As an example, Google Now pulls in data from your Google account to offer suggestions about local activities, weather updates, and news items of interest (see Figure 1.4).

User Interface

The user interface (UI) is the look and feel of an operating system. A good interface puts the user first, making commands and access to apps easy to discover. For the programmer, understanding how the interface works and what impact it has on application design is extremely useful.

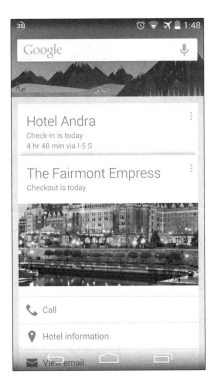

Figure 1.4   Google Now uses a variety of sources to pull out contextual data. Modern operating systems are constantly processing data in an attempt to anticipate the user's needs.

Android provides an interface that is easy to maneuver, with a home screen that can show apps or widgets (see Figure 1.5). A Google search bar is also present for easy access to both search and Google Now, the contextual information tool from Figure 1.4.

Because Android allows for significant amounts of customization, sometimes the UI varies from one device to another. For example, most of the major Android device manufacturers create a custom UI (sometimes referred to as a "skin"). So even though they are running Android, the icons and general look and feel of the operating system might be different on a Samsung device and one manufactured by LG or HTC.

Additionally, Android enables you to use a custom home screen launcher (see Figure 1.6).

Figure 1.5   The Android user interface.

Figure 1.6   The Yahoo! Aviate custom launcher.

Supported Android devices even allow the user to switch between different launchers (see Figure 1.7).

Fortunately, the apps built with App Inventor should not have much difficulty running on a variety of devices. Later, this book discusses how to test apps on specific devices, giving you the capability to troubleshoot any potential issues.

Android Strengths

Android has some specific advantages that make it a desirable operating system to write programs for. Because it is the world's most popular mobile operating system, app developers have the potential to reach a wide audience for their applications.

Android apps can be downloaded from the Google Play Store (see Figure 1.8). The web-based storefront and Play Store app on Android devices ensure that your application has wide visibility.

Google has also built in many services to Android that help developers, such as app usage statistics and the capability to upload apps without going through an approval process.

Figure 1.7   Android's settings enable the user to choose a custom launcher.

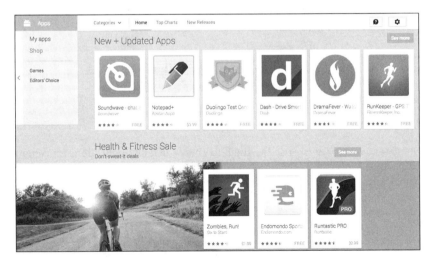

Figure 1.8   The Google Play Store hosts Android apps for users to download to their devices.

Extending App Capabilities

Android apps have access to more parts of the operating system (with user permission, of course), giving them additional power to access data from other apps than apps that are written for more closed systems, such as Apple's iOS. Android apps also have a great capability to interact with one another, which gives developers many choices. For example, Android's Intents feature allows an app to access the shared functionality of another app—for example, to use the built-in camera app or image-selection app from your app (see Figure 1.9).

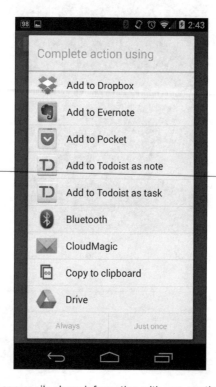

Figure 1.9   Android apps can easily share information with one another.

This flexibility extends to users, enabling them to choose default applications for certain procedures. For example, a user can open a web link in any browser or app that performs that function. As a developer, this is good news because it puts your app on fairly equal footing with other apps, even ones supplied with your Android device (see Figure 1.10).

Additionally, an app's capabilities can be extended to a home screen widget (as shown in Figure 1.11), which can display live, contextual information (currently, creating a widget with App Inventor is not possible). However, part of beginning to think like an app developer is to consider how an app could be extended to widgets and, as Android develops, wearable devices and TV.

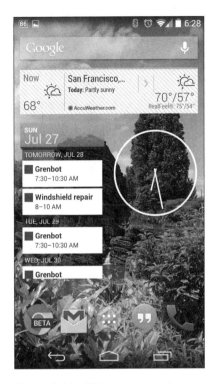

Figure 1.10   Android's Intents feature gives users more choice in what applications are tied to specific actions.

Figure 1.11   Widgets are another way of extending an app's utility to the home screen.

All of this opens up many possibilities when building applications. In the near term, you will focus primarily on just building a new app, but a later goal will be to maximize the use of Android to create an application that is a core part of the user experience.

Google Services

Google has increasingly built deeper ties to its own services with each iteration of Android. When signing in to an Android device, users log into their Google account, which may sync their device with their Gmail, Drive, Chrome, Maps data, and other Google services. Android now includes a large suite of native Google apps (see Figure 1.12).

Similarly, your Google account is an important part of using App Inventor: You need it to sign in and connect to Google Play if you plan to submit your apps for distribution in the Android storefront.

Figure 1.12   Google's core suite of apps is a key component of Android. Interacting with Google services can make for more powerful applications.

Google's development pace with Android is fairly rapid, and the company continues to forge deeper ties to Google services. Fortunately, as a programmer, you gain additional access to the power of Google-powered data with applications.

Because Android continues to put Google services front and center, thinking about how to complement these services is a good strategy for making successful apps. In Chapter 11, "Databases," we explore how to connect to other web services, to make your app a better source of information for the user.

Applications

The popularity of the smartphone brought about the concept of applications, or apps, as they have now come to be called (see Figure 1.13). The term *application* has always described a program that provides an interactive user experience for a certain task. Now the culturally new term *app*, along with its existence on phones, has democratized both their use and public interest in computing.

Figure 1.13   Smartphone owners expect a diversity of quality apps to download to their devices.

Android users can download apps through the Google Play Store (refer to Figure 1.8). With MIT App Inventor, you can build apps that you can then make available through Android's storefront.

App capabilities have become more complex in the area of multitasking. Android allows apps to run certain processes in the background after the user has switched to a different app. As you become more adept at building applications, identifying processes that will need to continue to run even if the app is in the background (such as playing an MP3 file or tracking the current location using GPS) will be an important part of the programming process (see Figure 1.14).

Programming Languages

Learning the intricacies of traditional, text-based programming languages has been a significant barrier for many people who want to learn application programming. App Inventor, however, was designed to address those barriers. It simplifies the programming process and enables the aspiring programmer to focus on the goals of the app.

Figure 1.14   The Android multitasking menu. As with other Android features, the look might differ slightly, depending on the custom UI running on a specific device.

The visual programming language you will learn in App Inventor provides a rapid entry point to programming Android applications. It serves as an excellent introduction if your goal is to eventually learn a traditional programming language such as Java or Objective-C. Even if you want to go no further, it is an excellent way to learn more about how mobile devices and applications interact with one another.

Another strength of visual programming is that it can serve as a bridge to using the current repertoire of developer tools. After mastering App Inventor, you will be better prepared for more advanced programming, such as using the Android Software Development Kit (SDK) and a program such as Android Studio for building an Android app (see Figure 1.15).

Additionally, the kind of thinking visual programming requires is helpful for many different lines of work. The problem solving and logical reasoning needed for programming is a highly desirable skill in the current economy.

No matter what your future path turns out to be, having a basic understanding of programming languages, operating systems, and computing devices will make the apps you create with MIT App Inventor more effective.

Figure 1.15   After you have mastered using App Inventor, it might be time to take the next step and get the Android SDK so that you can begin building more powerful and complicated applications.

Summary

Programming is what makes a well-designed application look like it performs magic. MIT App Inventor enables you to begin writing apps for Android very quickly, thanks to its low barrier for entry. After further practice and experimentation, you will be able to create apps of greater utility and complexity (see Figure 1.16). In fact, many apps in the Google Play Store have been created using App Inventor.

The next step after this survey of the structure of operating systems and applications is to learn the basics of the App Inventor program. We explore what it offers and how to get started using it to build apps.

The next chapter covers how to build an app with App Inventor and walks you through the first steps in doing so. Along the way, you will see how the computer science principles discussed in this chapter work in practice.

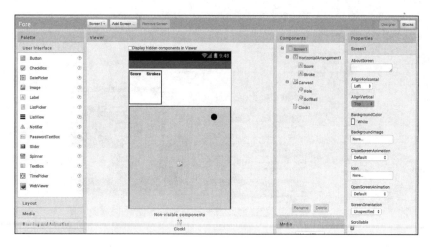

Figure 1.16   You can create games, animation, and a variety of apps when you use App Inventor to its full potential.

Exercises

Google has created an excellent resource for Android developers at developer.android.com. Here are a few areas to explore, to get a better feel for what good Android application design and development looks like (see Figure 1.17).

1. Application design and programming requires creative thinking just as much as reason and logic. Explore the Creative Vision section of the Android developer site: http://developer.android.com/design/get-started/creative-vision.html. Explore what design principles Google is looking for in apps built on the Android platform.

2. This chapter discussed some elements of the user interface, but you can also explore what Google has to say about it: http://developer.android.com/design/get-started/ui-overview.html.

3. Take a moment to examine the MIT App Inventor site: http://appinventor.mit.edu. Check out the Blog and Support sections to discover the resources available. Soon you will begin working in more depth with App Inventor and will begin building your own apps.

Figure 1.17   The Android developer site has considerable resources.

2

Building with MIT App Inventor

Understanding the functionality of an app is only one part of programming. The programmer also has to focus on specific features and how to implement them.

Before the serious work of building apps begins, a brief overview of how applications perform is useful. Let's get beyond the pretty screen and graphics that you interact with and start to look at what is really happening and how to make an app perform the way you envision. After doing this, you will be able to understand how apps can request information, pull in data from the Internet, and interact with other applications.

The MIT App Inventor Site

MIT App Inventor lives on the Web, just like other online productivity tools such as Gmail and Google Drive. You do not need to download any software or save work to your hard drive before you use App Inventor (see Figure 2.1).

The choice of web browser is very important; the App Inventor team recommends using Google Chrome or Firefox. Choosing a different browser, such as Internet Explorer, could result in errors or other complications when working with App Inventor.

Exploring the App Inventor site is a good way to get a feel for what is available. To begin, launch your browser and go to appinventor.mit.edu (see Figure 2.2). The home page includes the portal to the App Inventor tool, along with many online tutorials and other helpful materials.

Figure 2.1   The Designer interface in MIT App Inventor.

Signing In

To begin a session with App Inventor, click the Create button at the top of the home page (see Figure 2.2).

Figure 2.2   The App Inventor home page—click Create to get started.

Next, App Inventor asks permission to connect to your Google account. This can be a personal Google account (one that ends with an @gmail.com address) or a Google apps account managed by a university, business, or other type of organization (see Figure 2.3).

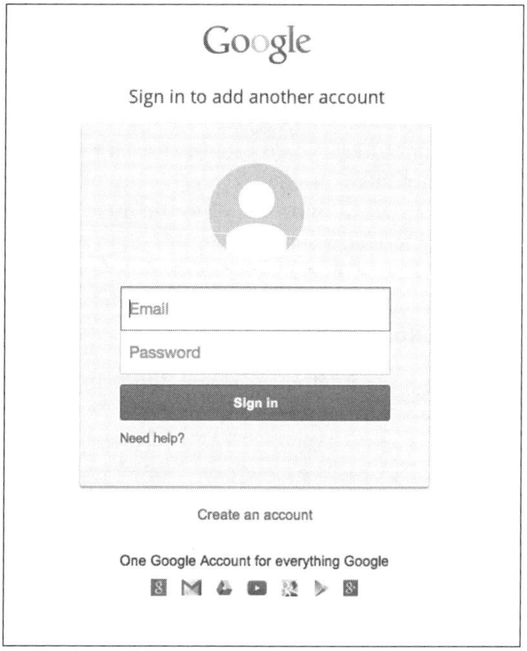

Figure 2.3   Add your Google account to connect to App Inventor.

After signing in with your Google account, you must authorize App Inventor to access your Google account so that it can verify your login information. If you select Remember This Approval for the Next 30 Days, then you will not need to repeat this step when you return to work on apps (see Figure 2.4). At the end of the 30 days, you simply need to reauthorize access.

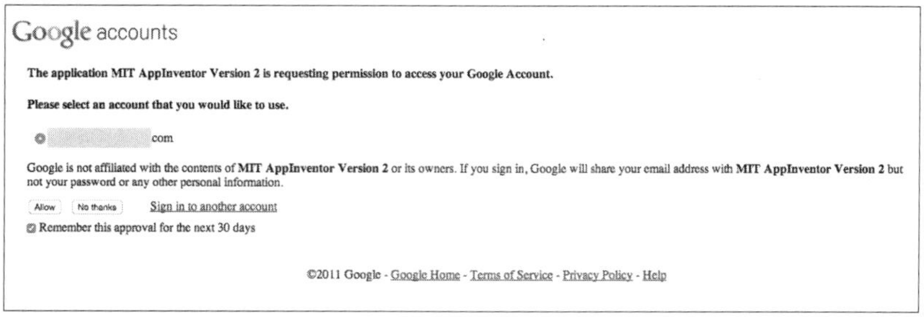

Figure 2.4   Authorize your Google account.

The next screen is the file system where App Inventor projects are stored. As you create more projects over time, you can find them there, just as a folder on your computer holds a list of all your documents saved to that location.

Next, click New Project and then type **CatWatch** into the box (spaces are not allowed). This takes you to the Designer screen.

Designer

App building begins in the Designer. Here you create the user interface, or the "look and feel" of the app. You also add the components needed to receive input from the user, as well as the components needed to display output or information to the user. The Designer also is where you specify which nonvisible components the app will use, such as the dialer, GPS, or SMS. Notice that because we are in Designer, the Designer button in Figure 2.5 is slightly grayed out in the top-right corner of the screen. This button, along with the one next to it, labeled Blocks, indicates which editor you are using.

The left side of the screen features the Palette (see Figure 2.5), which, as the name implies, is the space for all the creation tools (the next chapter details the full suite).

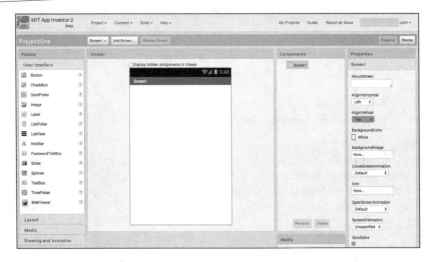

Figure 2.5   The App Inventor Designer screen.

Blocks Editor

The Blocks Editor is where you will be programming an app's behavior (see Figure 2.6). Here you will add the commands that do the work of the app. As just noted, you access it from the Blocks button at the top right.

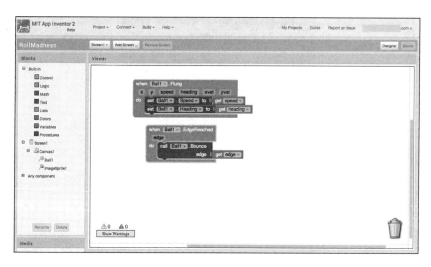

Figure 2.6   More specific programming takes place in the Blocks Editor.

MIT App Inventor uses the metaphor of drawers containing puzzle pieces for programming. Each item in the Blocks palette under Built-in is considered a drawer. The drawers contain the puzzle-looking pieces. The programming is accomplished by connecting the puzzle-looking pieces. Despite its seeming simplicity, App Inventor has many powerful capabilities that enable the user to build complex applications.

To better understand what programming an app entails, it is useful to understand what is going on inside an application.

The AI2 Companion App

App Inventor has a useful tool for continuously seeing your app in real time on an Android device during each step of the development process.

You can find the MIT AI2 Companion app (see Figure 2.7) in the Google Play Store by performing a search for "MIT AI2 Companion."

When you are building your app, the computer and Android device must be connected to the same wireless network (the desktop machine might have a wired connection). To connect your app to your device in App Inventor on your computer, click AI Companion on the Connect tab (see Figure 2.8).

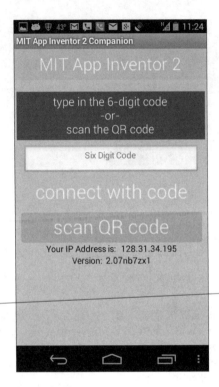

Figure 2.7   The AI2 Companion Android app.

Figure 2.8   Connecting to the Companion app.

You can then type in a six-digit code or scan the QR code with your device (see Figure 2.9), using the App Inventor app. Doing so brings up a live view of your app. As you add elements to it with the MIT App Inventor software, those changes are reflected in real time on your device.

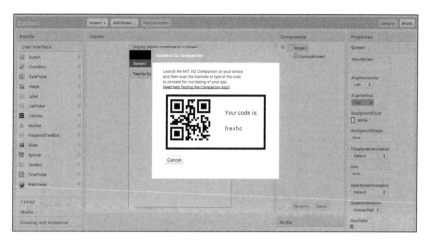

Figure 2.9   Connecting to the Companion app.

The Android Emulator

As another option, App Inventor has an Android emulator that puts a simulated Android screen on the computer desktop. This enables you to view the app's progression if you do not have an Android device. It also is useful for anyone using App Inventor in a classroom environment.

An installer package is available for Windows or Mac. Choose the proper platform from the App Inventor site and download it to your computer (see Figure 2.10).

To view your app, choose Emulator from the same menu in Figure 2.8.

USB Connection to Android Device

Another option is to connect your device to the computer with a USB cable. This method provides the benefit of seeing the app on your Android device just as if you were using the MIT App Inventor Emulator application. This option also does not require a wireless network connection (see Figure 2.11).

First, you need to install the App Inventor setup software to your Mac or Windows PC. Many Android devices also require the installation of driver software (available at the device manufacturer's website). Your device might require other changes to the device's settings. Android has a web page that describes the potential changes and implications at http://appinventor.mit.edu/explore/ai2/setup-device-wifi.html.

After you have properly configured your device, select Connect and choose USB from the menu. After a few moments, the app should appear live on your device.

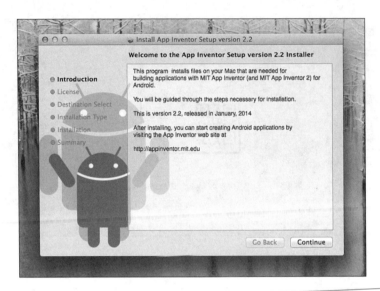

Figure 2.10   The emulator download package. The emulator can be downloaded to a Mac or a Windows PC.

Figure 2.11   The Android emulator.

Getting Inside an App

Apps have an internal design, the programming that works with the user interface. Effective programming entails knowing how to use the internal components to effectively implement what is visible to the user.

A good way to think about the internal pieces of an app is to focus on components and actions. The components are the various tools you find in App Inventor to create tasks. Think about the Design Editor and all the onscreen tools: buttons, images, drawings, and so on. In the Design Editor, you pull into your app all the pieces that make up the user interface, or what the users of your app will see on the device's screen.

Event Handlers

All of your blocks, the pieces that make your app perform tasks, will be connected with an event handler. Events are created whenever something in the real world happens to the app, such as when the user clicks a button, the phone's location changes, or the phone receives a text message. Blocks exist for just about everything you want to do in an app; taking a picture, checking the GPS location, displaying text, changing the color of a component, finding out what the user entered into a text box, and so on. You can add (or remove) these blocks from an event handler, allowing the programming to determine the precise set of actions to take when the user presses a button.

When any event happens, App Inventor runs whatever blocks are inside the **event handler** block for that event. For example, Figure 2.12 shows a button labeled Speak; the block **when Speak.Click do** is the event handler for when that button is clicked.

Imagine that we wanted to write an app to speak written text. We would need a button to start the process. To do this, we would have to drag the **action** block into the event handler. Whenever the button is clicked, that block will be called, and the device will move to whatever blocks have been placed inside the event handler. The event handler will grow and shrink as needed to accommodate whatever blocks are placed inside it (in Figure 2.13, this involves speaking some text). The way it is right now, however, the app has a button and a text-to-speech component, but it won't do anything because the event handler is empty. After we drag in some action blocks, it will do those actions whenever the button is clicked. Note that the component used to initiate the action (such as a button) is usually different than the component that does the requested action (such as taking a picture or sending a text message).

when Speak.Click do action block

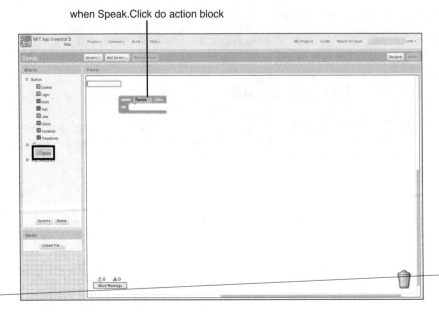

Figure 2.12   An event handler in the Blocks Editor.

Figure 2.13   An event handler.

Doing One Thing at a Time

Modern smartphone applications perform a large number of tasks simultaneously—or at least appear to do so. All computers, including smartphones, are so good at switching between different tasks so quickly that it appears they are doing two unrelated things simultaneously.

Many computers have multiple cores, or processing units. These computers really can do more than one thing because each core can work on a separate task. But those cores are also switching very quickly between many tasks that the system and user are trying to do. You might have two, or four, or even more separate cores in your computer or phone, but between the operating system and the apps, the processor has hundreds of small tasks to work on.

Most of the things you will do in App Inventor are single task, meaning that only one task is actually running at a time. However, they can happen quickly and get out of the way for other things to run. In the code blocks, *only one event handler can run at a time*. So when an event happens and the event handler begins executing the blocks you put in it, all other event handlers must wait until this one is done.

Events that take place while a handler is already running are put in a queue and will run when it is their turn. Most event handlers run much faster than events are generated, so this is often not an issue. The most common actions, such as updating the text in a label or looking at the state of a check box, occur nearly instantly. However, other actions, such as working through a large collection of data, might take a long time, and the app will appear frozen until the process finishes.

While an event handler is running, the display isn't updated. Again, this isn't an issue most of the time, but if you have an event handler that is taking long enough for a user to notice, the display will appear frozen until the event handler is complete.

You might notice that some features in App Inventor take time, such as playing sounds or music. Other features have to wait for something on the Internet to respond, which can cause an unpredictable amount of delay time. But the display doesn't freeze when you play music, and the app continues to work while waiting for a web page to load. Android provides the means to allow some tasks, such as playing music, to run in the background without disrupting the normal actions your app performs. Android provides other means of dealing with actions that could take a long time, or that might never finish, such as loading a web page or waiting for the user to take a picture, without affecting the normal functioning of your app. The actions for music and sound are made possible by the Android system. Your app simply hands off the sound file to the phone's operating system and tells the phone to handle it. The music plays while the app continues to work.

Later in the text, we provide more details on how App Inventor switches tasks. You can use that knowledge to make better apps.

Exercise: Sherlock Is Watching

Next we create an app that uses some of the basic functionality described in this section. As with the other apps you will build in this book, there is flexibility in the specifics. Feel free to experiment after following the steps to get a feel for how all the pieces work and the type of customizations possible. Learning to build apps is a process that involves both following the step-by-step directions and branching out on your own.

1. Navigate back to your projects by clicking My Projects at the top of the page (see Figure 2.14).

2. If you created a CatWatch app earlier, select it from your list of projects; otherwise, create a new project called CatWatch.

3. Click User Interface in the Palette. The Palette then expands to reveal several choices, such as Button, Checkbox, and Clock. Click and hold the Button choice, and then drag it onto the Android home screen in the Viewer (see Figure 2.15). A button appears in the Viewer, indicating that an element has been added to the screen. The button's name also is added to the Components tree.

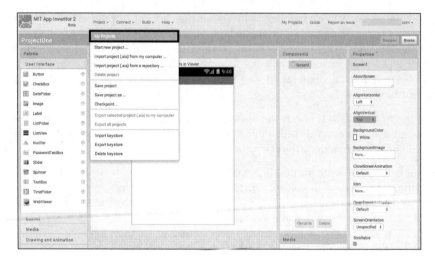

Figure 2.14   The My Projects button is for creating new projects and accessing existing ones.

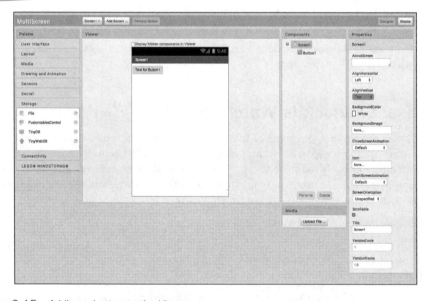

Figure 2.15   Adding a button to the Viewer.

4. The button shows with the following default text: Text for Button1. Let's change the name of the button. Click the label in either the Viewer or the Components tree and then click the Rename button. In the box that launches, give it another name, such as Meow.

5. Notice that changing the name of the button does not change the button's text. To change the displayed text, click the button and then find the box labeled Text inside the Properties pane. Then highlight the text and type Meow. The text will change in the Viewer.

Adding an Image

Images are an effective way to add some visual polish to an app. Next, we insert an image into the app.

1. If you have not done so already, download the CatIsWatching image from the book's InformIT page.

2. Find the box labeled Media, which is just below the Components box. Click the Upload File button (see Figure 2.16) and then upload the CatIsWatching file. This adds the image to the app, making it available to any component that uses the image. Note that the filename appears in the media box.

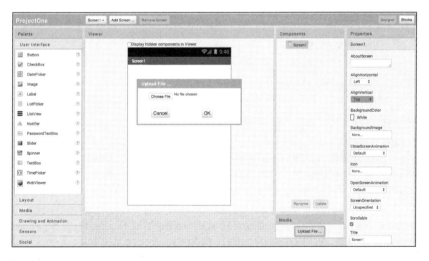

Figure 2.16   Uploading an image.

3. Click User Interface in the Palette. Then click and hold the image and drag it onto the Android home screen in the Viewer. A blue bar shows where you can place the image. By moving the mouse, you can place the image above or below the Button. When the blue bar is below the Button, drop the image. Next click the Image1 button in the Components box. The Properties pane updates to display the properties associated with the image.

4. Click the box labeled Picture. All available images in your app are listed; select the CatIsWatching image. Click OK to see the image appear in the Viewer (see Figure 2.17).

Figure 2.17   Uploading an image.

5. The image of Sherlock the cat needs to be tweaked to properly fill the screen. Click in the width box and then click the box that reads Pixels. Type **320** pixels.

6. The procedure is the same for the height: Click the height box and then type **400** pixels.

7. This app requires one more element. From User Interface, click and drag the Label component. Again, watching the blue insertion bar, drop the Label between the button and the Image components. Next, select Label1 in the Components box. Click the button underneath the BackgroundColor label, which is currently set to None. Then choose Green.

8. It is time to write some text inside the box. Go to the Text box and type **Sherlock is watching**. Choose TextAlignment and change this selection to Center. Notice that this does not change the position of the label—it changes only the text inside it (see Figure 2.18).

9. Click Blocks in the upper-right corner. You should see Meow, Label1, and Image1 underneath Screen1. This is where you would drag these components into the Blocks Editor for further programming.

This first app is relatively simple, but it should make you feel more familiar with the core pieces of App Inventor. Later apps will make more extensive use of the interface elements and how they can be programmed. We will also explore how to put this app on your own device and interact with it.

Figure 2.18 The completed image and label.

What Can You Build?

This first exercise demonstrates a little of what is possible with App Inventor. Throughout this book, you will learn how to maximize the power of App Inventor to build a variety of apps.

The skills you gain will also empower you to begin your own experimentation and build apps beyond the walk-throughs provided in this text.

The following sections preview some of the other apps and exercises we will be exploring throughout the book. With careful attention to detail and some creativity, you will be able to build these apps and have the foundations for creating your own set of applications.

Speak, Android!

Give your Android device a voice. This simple app (see Figure 2.19) teaches you how to enable an image to respond to touch and speak on command. You can also use it to explore other ways to work with images.

Pollock

Named after Jackson Pollock, the American artist who helped popularize abstract art, this app turns an Android device into a canvas for color (see Figure 2.20). You will learn how to turn buttons into paint and use the Canvas component.

Figure 2.19   The Speak, Android app.

Figure 2.20   The Pollock app.

Fore

MIT App Inventor has some surprisingly powerful tools for creating games. Various motion-enabled commands enable you to create some powerful games. The game you will be building will show how you can use the canvas and various sprites to create a game field and objects that can be manipulated while playing (see Figure 2.21).

Android Quiz

Games can be fun to create, but imagine being able to use an app for your own productivity. Android Quiz (see Figure 2.22) demonstrates that you can create an actual assessment app.

Uploading to Google Play

Later chapters discuss several ways to share your app with others. However, the ultimate step is uploading your app to Google Play for distribution to other Android users.

Figure 2.21   The Fore golf game.   Figure 2.22   Android Quiz.

Summary

MIT App Inventor is a powerful tool that beginning coders or anyone dabbling with mobile technology can use to build Android apps. In this chapter, we looked at the kind of apps that are possible with this cloud-based tool.

Computer science is applied reasoning using both art and science. It requires the ability to communicate ideas through a combination of language and powerful technology. Hopefully this first app has demonstrated that App Inventor is an excellent starting point for anyone looking to create with computer technology, whether professionally or recreationally.

In the next chapter, we build an app that includes both an image and sound, and we look at how to see the app on your own device.

Exercises

1. Add another button to the Viewer. Change the text, trying different configurations to see how they fit in the Viewer.

2. Upload a different image. Download one from the Web or upload an image on your computer. Try different configurations for size in relation to the rest of the app. Decide on the optimal size for images in the context of the rest of the content.

3. Change the text and color scheme in the label. Try labels in different locations of the app. Pay attention to how the Designer works in terms of the placement of components and how you can customize the components.

3

App Inventor Toolkit

App building with MIT App Inventor begins with the Designer (see Figure 3.1). This is where you will choose the general capabilities and design for your application.

The Designer has a user-friendly method for adding features to your app. You can drag and drop the various tools, called components, onto a virtual Android device screen.

These components all have specific capabilities that perform any number of tasks. As you continue to build with MIT App Inventor, it will be useful to try out various components and experiment with how they can impact an app's function. As you become more familiar with the components, you will find a variety of new and innovative ways to add them into your apps.

In this chapter, you learn the basics of the Designer screen and how to create your very first app. The Designer is where you build the visual look of your app—and learn about some of its key features along the way.

Building the app Speak, Android! also requires use of the Blocks Editor, which is where you add the commands that do the work of the app. You learn how to upload an image and use the text-to-speech function, making your app "speak" to you.

At the conclusion of this chapter, you should feel confident in navigating the Designer screen, adding images, and experimenting with the various components available.

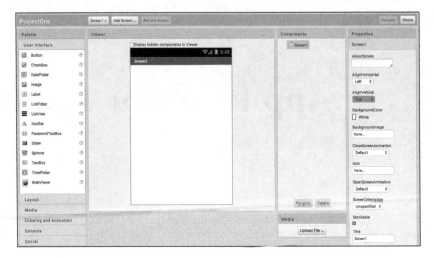

Figure 3.1   The App Inventor Designer. The components on the left side of the screen help you build the functions of your app.

Creating a New Project

Log in to the MIT App Inventor 2 site and click the Projects tab to start a new project.

A box appears requesting a project name. Type **Speak** into the box and press the OK button.

App Inventor has some specific naming requirements: Project names must start with a letter and can contain only letters, numbers, and underscores. In addition, you cannot have a space between two words.

After you enter the name of a project, you are taken to the Designer screen. This screen is the first of two core areas where you do the design work of building apps, creating the apps' look and feel. The second area is the Blocks Editor (accessed through the Blocks button at the top right), where you add the commands to perform the apps' tasks. You will use this section as you create the first app, with a more thorough exploration in future apps and chapters.

Designer Essentials

The Designer screen has several sections you want to become familiar with: the Palette, Viewer, Components, Media, and Properties sections.

Even though MIT App Inventor does not require using code in the traditional sense, some of the concepts covered here are very detailed and technical, so learning how they work and impact the other pieces of your app is important.

Palette

The Palette (see Figure 3.2) is where you add all the elements that make the app perform any number of tasks. The components are grouped by functionality, making it easy to find the right component. As you can see in Figure 3.2, the first element is the User Interface element.

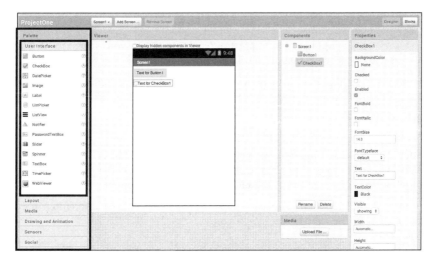

Figure 3.2   The Palette section.

The rest of this section briefly explores each component and summarizes its specific purpose within MIT App Inventor. The program provides even more details about each of these components. For further information about how you can use these components with your app, click the question mark icon next to the one you want to explore.

User Interface

The User Interface element holds several components that are essential to building your app. This section provides a brief overview of what they do. However, the best way to learn the various pieces of any tool such as MIT App Inventor is to try them out. Note that all the components in this group have visual aspects, such as text color and font size, that you can change either in the Designer when creating the app or as the app is running using commands available in the Blocks Editor.

- **Button**   This component adds a button that can be clicked with the user's finger. You can customize its appearance in a number of ways, including specifying whether it is clickable (this is enabled by default).

- **Checkbox**   The Checkbox raises an event when the user clicks it. You can use both the Designer Editor and the Blocks Editor to customize its appearance.

- **DatePicker**   This is a button that, when clicked, launches a popup dialog so the user can select a date.

- **Image**   This component adds images to your app. You can customize the specific image and its appearance using either the Designer Editor or the Blocks Editor.

- **Label**   A label displays a piece of text that can give further organization to your app.

- **ListPicker**   This button displays a list of text elements for the user to choose from.

- **ListView**   This component places a list of text elements on your screen for display. It will not work on screens that are scrollable.

- **Notifier**   This component displays a notification. You can customize how it appears and what kind of information it will save through the Android log entries.

- **PasswordTextBox**   With this component, you can create a text box that will not display the characters when the user types them into the box.

- **Slider**   The slider is a progress bar that adds a dragable thumb. When touched, the slider can be dragged to the left or right. Doing so impacts another component attribute, such as the font size of a TextBox or the radius of the Ball component.

- **Spinner**   This component displays a pop-up menu with a list of different elements. You can set these in the Designer or Blocks Editor.

- **TextBox**   As its name implies, this is a box for text. You can customize whether the text box has multiple lines and whether it is restricted to numbers, among other specific features.

- **WebViewer**   This creates a component for viewing web pages inside the app, without sending the user to an external browser.

Layout

The layout can greatly influence the look and feel of your app. The Layout section presents you with three different configuration options (see Figure 3.3):

- **Horizontal Arrangement**   If you drag this component onto your screen, any other elements you place inside will be arranged horizontally.

- **Table Arrangement**   The components will be arranged next to one another, as in a table.

- **Vertical Arrangement**   The components will be arranged vertically.

Media

Many Android applications today make extensive use of various forms of media. MIT App Inventor gives you many choices for including video, images, or sound (see Figure 3.4). These components enable you to create an app that can access the device's video recorder or camera. This is also where you add your own images, a fairly frequent occurrence in most apps.

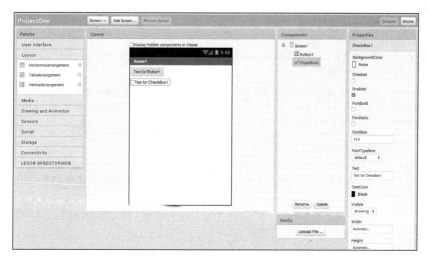

Figure 3.3   App Inventor provides three layout choices for components.

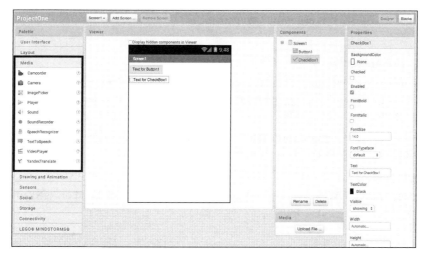

Figure 3.4   The Media components.

The following options are available to you from the Media section:

- **Camcorder**   The Camcorder accesses your device's video recorder, enabling the user to make a recording while using your app.

- **Camera**   Just like the Camcorder, this element accesses the camera and allows you to enable picture taking from inside the app.

- **ImagePicker**   This tool makes it possible for users to import an image from their device. When this button is selected, the device's gallery appears and an image can be selected.

- **Player**   This is a multimedia component that plays audio and video and also controls the phone's vibration.

- **Sound**   This component plays sound files and vibrates for a specified number of milliseconds if specified in the Blocks Editor. MIT App Inventor recommends this for shorter sound files, such as sound effects.

- **Sound Recorder**   This component records audio.

- **Speech Recognizer**   This component is useful for giving the user the capability to speak into the device's microphone and have it recognized by the app, commonly known as speech to text.

- **Text to Speech**   With this component, your app can "speak" to a user by turning text into spoken audio.

- **Video Player**   This multimedia component can play videos. Commands for play, pause, and skip ahead also appear when the user plays a video.

- **Yandex Translate**   This component uses the Yandex translation service to translate words and phrases among different languages. Be sure your test device is online when trying any app that is using this component.

Drawing and Animation

App Inventor has several components that enable the user to draw or interact with animation inside the app (see Figure 3.5). We use these in one of our sample apps later in the text. The components include the following:

- **Ball**   The ball is a round sprite (an interactive image) that can react to touches, drags, and interactions with other such sprites.

- **Canvas**   The canvas is a touch-sensitive area where you can add sprites.

- **Image Sprite**   Just like a ball, this is a sprite that can be touched and dragged and can also interact with other sprites.

Sensors

The sensors are components that interact with some of the hardware features on an Android device. For example, these are useful when building an app that interacts with a user's location, device movement, or other hardware through Near Field Communication (see Figure 3.6). The types of sensors include the following:

- **Accelerometer Sensor**   The accelerometer is hardware built into the device that can measure movement.

- **Bar Code Scanner**   This component enables the app to read bar codes. This has become popular in shopping apps for comparing products and prices across various storefronts.

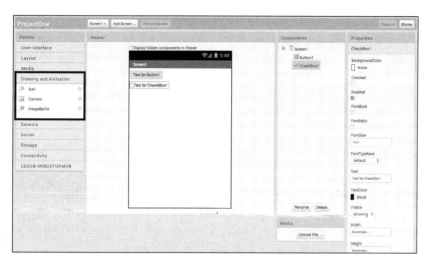

Figure 3.5   The Drawing and Animation components.

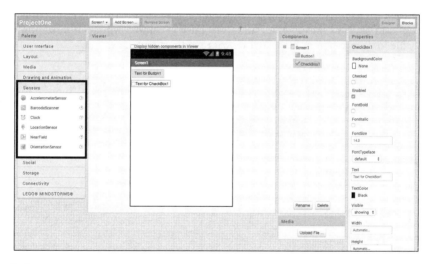

Figure 3.6   The Sensors components.

- **Location Scanner**   Apps can access the device's location with this component.
- **Near Field**   This component makes use of Near Field Communication (NFC).
- **Orientation Sensor**   This nonvisible component gives information about the device's physical orientation, based on its roll, pitch, or azimuth.

Social

Some apps are social in nature, geared to sending messages or interacting with your contacts. These components (see Figure 3.7) enable you to connect the app to a user's contacts for email or phone calls:

- **Contact Picker**   This button displays a list of contacts. The user can then select a contact from the device's address book and see a name, email address, or picture, depending on how you configure this.

- **Email Picker**   This component creates a text box where a user can enter an email address of a contact. The box uses autosuggest if the contact is already in the device's address book.

- **Phone Call**   This component makes a phone call to a specified number.

- **Phone Number Picker**   When this button is clicked, it displays a list of contacts' phone numbers.

- **Sharing**   This launches the Android share option, allowing users to send their content to another app.

- **Texting**   This component allows users to send a text message from an app.

- **Twitter**   This nonvisible dialog allows communication with Twitter. To use it, however, you must obtain a Consumer Key and Consumer Secret for Twitter authorization that is specific to your app from http://twitter.com/oauth_clients/new.

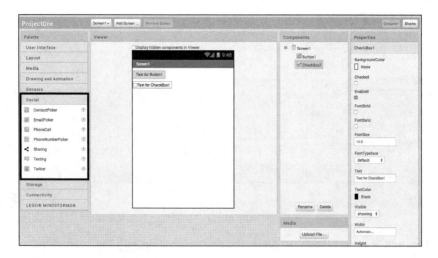

Figure 3.7   The Social components

Storage

The following components interact with data and storage, so you can create an app that saves information on the device and interacts with any collected data (see Figure 3.8).

- **File**   This is a hidden component for storing and retrieving files.

- **Fusion Tables Control**   This nonvisible component communicates with Google Fusion Tables, which enable you to store, share, query, and visualize data tables.

- **TinyDB**   This component stores data for an app.

- **TinyWebDB**   The TinyWebDB communicates with a web service to store and receive information.

Figure 3.8   You can access storage with these components.

Connectivity

This component can launch a variety of different activities (see Figure 3.9), including performing a web search, starting the camera, and opening another app that was built with App Inventor. Two Bluetooth components also enable an app to connect with Bluetooth devices. The following list briefly explains the four activities:

- **ActivityStarter**   This launches any kind of activity that uses the·**StartActivity** command. It can start other App Inventor apps, start a camera application, perform a web search, open a browser to a specific page, or open a map to a specified location.

- **BluetoothClient** This provides the names and addresses of paired Bluetooth devices and indicates whether Bluetooth is enabled.

- **BluetoothServer** The BluetoothServer component indicates whether there is an incoming connection and whether one has been made.

- **Web** This invisible component has functions for HTTP, GET, POST, PUT, and DELETE requests.

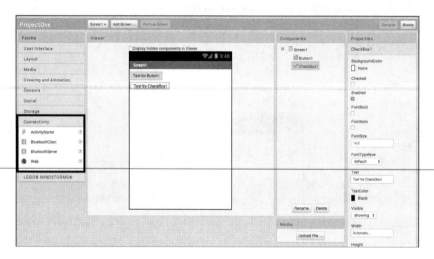

Figure 3.9   The Connectivity components

LEGO MINDSTORMS

MIT App Inventor supports several components for use with LEGO MINDSTORMS NXT robots programming (see Figure 3.10). The LEGO components interact with the various sensors that can be built into an NXT robot.

Viewer

The Viewer is where you drag out the components (see Figure 3.11). It provides a view of what you have built into the app, with a modest expectation of how it might look.

A check box just above the Viewer displays any components that would generally be hidden. In later applications, you will see how this can be useful in ensuring the reliability of an app.

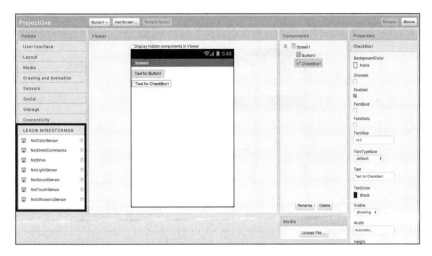

Figure 3.10   The LEGO MINDSTORMS components.

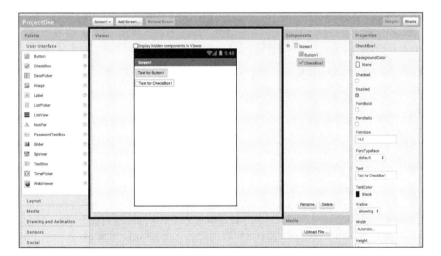

Figure 3.11   The Viewer is the mock Android screen where you drag components.

Components

The Components box displays all the components that have been added to the app (see Figure 3.12). A list of components is nested under the screen in which the components were placed. These lists can be expanded or collapsed to focus on the components from a specific screen.

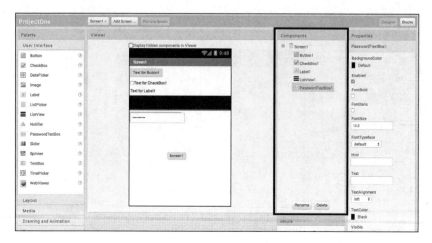

Figure 3.12   All of the included components appear in this box. From here, you can make further customizations for components that offer this.

Click once on a component to highlight it. From here, the options are to delete the component (by pressing the Delete button) or rename it. When you press the Rename button, a box appears over the component's name; you can type a different name for it in that box.

When highlighting a component, the Properties box changes to reflect its various configuration options.

Properties

The Properties box contains the configuration options available in each component (see Figure 3.13).

When you click on one of the components in either the Viewer or the Components box, all the specific options for that component will be available there. For example, when you click a button, you can change its default color, the font size, the typeface, and the text alignment. Properties are also available for each screen that enable you to customize the screen orientation, alignment, and background color, as well as make other tweaks.

Media

In the Media box (not to be confused with the Media components in the Palette), you upload any images or other media files to be used in the app. Click on Upload File to open a dialog box that can import any media file from your computer.

The image then appears in the Viewer window. You can click on it to access some of the customization options or delete it.

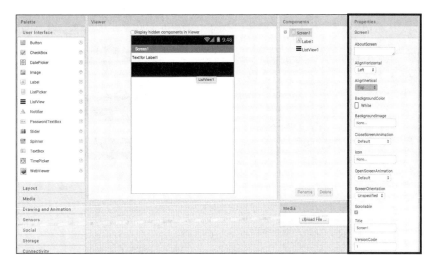

Figure 3.13   In the Properties box, you can make adjustments and customizations to the components.

Exercise: Speak, Android!

It is time to create another app. This app, which we call Speak, Android!, will say a specific phrase when an icon is touched. We use the Designer and the Blocks Editor to manipulate an image.

1. Click on Project and select Start New Project (see Figure 3.14). In the pop-up box, type **SpeakAndroid** and click OK.

2. Next, you are on the Designer screen. The first component needed is Button, located in the User Interface box. Click and hold the button and drag it to the Viewer. When you release, the box will be in the Viewer and will display the words **Text for Button1**. Now we can change the name of the button. It's always a good idea to give your components a descriptive name. Click Rename Button at the bottom on the Component box and give the component a new name of Speak.

3. Now we will change the text that is displayed for this button. Click inside the Text box in the Properties box and highlight the existing text, which currently says, **Text for Button1**.

4. Type **I speak!**. Notice that the text on the button in the Viewer changes as well. Such adjustments are also easier to monitor from one of the emulation options available from MIT App Inventor.

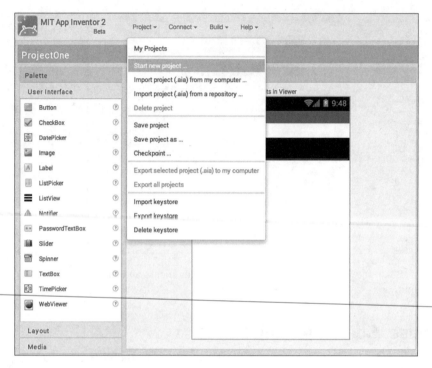

Figure 3.14   Begin a new project by selecting Start New Project.

Connecting Your Device

As you build this app, you can more easily keep track of its development by seeing how it looks in real time.

The recommended method for doing this, as discussed in Chapter 2, "Building with MIT App Inventor," is to install the MIT AI2 Companion app on an Android device (see Figure 3.15). You can find it in the Google Play Store by performing a search for "MIT AI2 Companion." Be sure to download this specific version—the MIT App Inventor Version 1 app will not work with the apps you build in this text.

You also can download the app directly without going through the Google Play Store. To do this, click the Connect tab at the top of the screen and then select AI Companion. A QR code launches that can be scanned with a QR Reader, such as Google Goggles.

Technically savvy users can then install the app directly on their device by downloading the **.apk** file. However, going this route means you must manually update the app because it will not be issued updates from the Google Play Store.

Figure 3.15　The MIT AI2 Companion Android app.

When building your app, the computer and Android device must be connected to the same wireless network. To connect your app to your device in App Inventor on your computer, click the AI Companion link from the Connect tab (see Figure 3.16).

You can then type in a six-digit code or scan the QR code with your device using the App Inventor app. Doing either brings up a live view of your app. As you add elements to it with the MIT App Inventor software, those changes will reflect in real time on your device.

As Chapter 2 discussed, if you do not have an Android device or you would rather do all your work on the computer screen, you have another option. App Inventor has an Android emulator that puts a simulated Android device on your desktop. To enable this, you must download the installer package for Windows or Mac. It is updated rather frequently, so be sure to monitor whether you have the most recent update when signing in to your account. Although this gives you a general sense of how the app looks, the most effective way to get a complete feel for how the app performs and its nuances is to use an Android device (the MIT App Inventor team also strongly recommends this).

Additionally, another option is to connect your device to the computer with a USB cord. This method (also discussed in Chapter 2) provides the benefits of seeing the app on your Android device, just as if you were using the MIT App Inventor Emulator application.

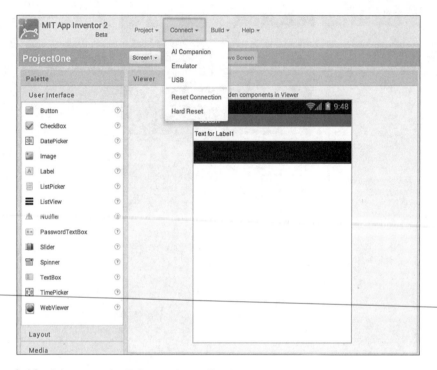

Figure 3.16   Connect to the AI Companion or Emulator.

First, you need to install the App Inventor Setup Software to your Mac or Windows PC. Some connections might not work if you don't have the correct drivers (third-party software for printers and other connections). However, most computers and other devices should function properly (MIT offers a test page to determine whether your connection is successful).

Then to make the connection, select Connect and USB. After a few moments, the app should appear live on your device.

See Your App on a Connected Device

Regardless of how you have chosen to connect your device, it should have an I Speak! button in the top-left corner of the screen (see Figure 3.17). Using the onscreen emulator, a USB connection, or the MIT App Inventor app, monitor the growth and changes to the app as you add functions.

Figure 3.17   A button as seen through the AI2 app.

Next, in the Design page, go to the Media section and drag the TextToSpeech component onto the Viewer. It will appear under the Nonvisible components area because it does not contain an image that will appear on a device (see Figure 3.18).

Now it's time to add a little flavor to the app by uploading an image.

1. Go to the book's page on InformIT and click the Downloads tab. Then download the ZIP file to your computer and unzip the Android icon to your computer.

2. Look in the Components table and select the Speak button that you created. Then go to Image in the Properties box and click Upload File. Select the Android image that you previously downloaded.

3. Next, you need to tweak the displayed image so that it looks properly centered on the screen. Select Width and change it to **330** pixels. Then change Height to **400** pixels.

4. To make the text pop, click the FontBold button in the Properties box. Now you should have an Android centered on the screen with the text I Speak! across the middle (see Figure 3.19). You might see slight variations in how it is positioned, depending on your device, but it should scale properly.

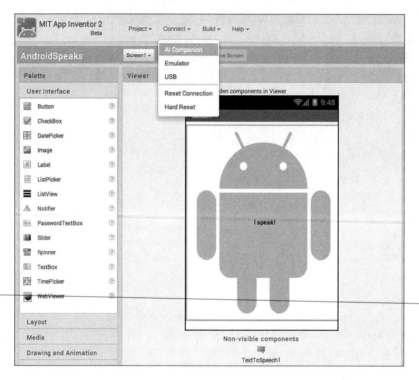

Figure 3.18   Both the AI Companion and Emulator let you see how your app is progressing.

Figure 3.19   The app as seen through the AI2 Companion.

5. To make the app speak, the text-to-speech function must be programmed. Doing so requires the Blocks Editor. Click the Blocks button in the upper-right side of the screen.

6. Then click the Speak button in the Blocks box, which pulls up several puzzle pieces to choose from (see Figure 3.20). Select the **when Speak.Click** event handler and drag it into the Viewer workspace.

Figure 3.20   Using the Blocks Editor in the app.

7. Next, select the TextToSpeech1 component and drag the **call TextToSpeech1.Speak** piece as well.

8. Finally, choose the Text drawer and select the empty text block at the top of the list. Drag it into the Viewer workspace and connect it to the right side of the **TextToSpeech.Speak** block. Now click in the oval opening in the text box and type **Well done, this is your first app**. (Any phrase will work, and feel free to experiment with different words after you complete the app.) Finally, drag the **TextToSpeech.Speak** block into the Speak event handler. Make sure the blocks connect; otherwise, App Inventor will not recognize the commands as part of the event handler.

9. Now, using your Companion app, press the Android and you will hear it say, "Well done, this is your first app!"

Before moving on, you might want to tweak some of the features that are built in, such as the size of the image, the text on the Android, or the words spoken by the text-to-speech component.

Summary

This Android Speaks app should give you a sense of what is capable with MIT App Inventor. It also serves as a good starting point for deciding what components to explore next, depending on what kind of apps you are thinking about building. Just with this first exercise, you might have explored some of the components or blocks and discovered far more capabilities than what you used in this first journey.

While progressing through the text, you will find more opportunities to practice with the core elements of MIT App Inventor, as well as explore the more sophisticated functions. The key is to continue to be willing to experiment and use the exercises as a starting place for trying out your own apps. You can tweak or customize each app and exercise in many different places, which will increase your own capabilities with App Inventor.

Exercises

1. Instead of using the Android image provided by the InformIT download, substitute your own image. Be sure that the blocks match how they were configured when you first built this app.

2. In the Blocks Editor, write different phrases in place of **Well done, this is your first app**. Experiment with the range of language App Inventor uses in converting text to speech.

3. Currently, the text on the button reads I Speak!—rename the text and use one of the different alignments in the Properties.

4

Variables

Think about what *variable* means in math. If you've done a little algebra, you're probably thinking of a letter that represents some number. The benefit of using a variable is that you can work with the letter without having to know what the number is. You might be able to figure out what the number is, but in many cases, you don't need to think about it. The letter representing a number is an *abstraction*. A value (a hard number) can be represented by a letter or a name, and then you don't have to think about the details of *what* the number is. If you know, for instance, that $x < 6$, you don't have to know exactly what x is. All you need to know is that x is less than 6. The details beyond that don't matter. It's no longer just a number; it's any possible number. Then you get to the best part: The equations and math you can do with a variable can be made to *always* work, even without knowing what value is actually in the variable. It could be any value; it doesn't matter to you anymore. You're no longer worried about individual *numbers*—all you care about is the simpler but more abstract idea of the variable, which is a *representation* of some number. That's a beautiful thing.

In computing, that meaning of *variable* is still true, but there's a little more to consider. First, a variable is usually not just a single letter. It can be any word or combination of letters. This means variables can have names that describe what they contain and what they're supposed to be used to do.

As in math, a variable in computing is a name representing a value. That value doesn't have to be a number. Maybe it's a selection of text. Maybe it's a color. Maybe it's just the answer to a yes/no question. In App Inventor, you can store *any kind of value* in a variable, not just numbers.

Here's a hard reality of programming: You, the programmer, get to see the code blocks only as a still photo, before they are run on the device. When the app is running on the device, the code is moving, crunching through events and data, but you don't get to see all that motion—you can see only the parts that *will* move. This is especially true when you go to use your app or distribute it to your users. That code will continue to run and churn long after you've stopped looking at the blocks. You have to write your code for it to move, but you see it only as a still image.

The good news is, variables are here to help you. A variable stores a value, and you can use that value in your code without ever knowing what the value is at any time.

Component Properties: The Built-in Variables

You have already seen that each component you have in your app has some collection of properties that are visible in the Designer screen. These properties control various traits of that particular component, including its color, the text it displays, and its shape, among many others. Each component has a set of parameters that are relevant to that type of component. A check box has the property **isChecked**, which describes, as you may guess, whether that check box is currently checked. No other component has the concept of being checked, so no other component has this property. But the check box does display some text, so it also has a **text** property, as do many other components.

All the properties you see in the Designer window are variables that are built into the components. You can change them in both the Designer *and* the code blocks. Changing properties in the Designer affects what their values will be when the app first starts up. Everything after that is controlled by the blocks, the user, and their interactions.

> **Note**
>
> A couple special properties are not accessible in the code blocks. They are in Screen1 and are named **VersionCode** and **VersionName**. Both can be set only manually by the programmer in the Designer. These properties manage the official app version and are used by the Google Play Store and the Android system to know when to update.

Clicker-Counter App

Consider an example: a Clicker-Counter app. Counting clickers are often used in theaters, auditoriums, and other large-group settings to count how many people enter; an attendant simply clicks a button for each person who comes in. We're going to make a basic counter, but it can be extended to count anything, or any number of things, like a baseball umpire's counter or a billiards scorekeeper.

All we need for this app is a single button. You might want to adjust its size properties to make it nice and big on the screen. For instance, you can set the width to Fill Parent and the height to 300 pixels. I renamed the button from Button1 to TheButton. You might also want to make the font size bigger and change the text to the number 0. If you make these modifications, it should look something like Figure 4.1.

The most important thing to do is set the text to **0**. That is our starting value for the counter, so *it must be a number*. We might as well make that number 0 because we haven't counted anything yet.

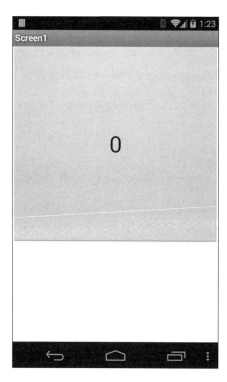

Figure 4.1 The big button of the Clicker-Counter app.

The interesting variable for this app is **TheButton.Text**, which is the text stored in and visible on TheButton. In that text, we have a start value, provided in the Designer, and we will have that value increase by 1 every time the button is clicked.

Properties: Getters and Setters

To use a component property as a variable, we need to be able to *get* the current value and *set* a new value. This is done with blocks called, logically, getters and setters. They are available in the flyout menu for each component (see Figure 4.2).

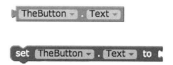

Figure 4.2 The getter and setter blocks for TheButton's **Text** property.

Here's the idea: Every time the button is clicked, we will *get* the current value that's in the text property, change it to be 1 greater, and then *set* that value back into the property. It will update the property to have the new number in it, which will appear on the screen.

That idea translates into blocks (see Figure 4.3). To make this work, you need to recruit the **addition** block and the **number** block from the Math built-in menu. The **number** block starts with a 0, and you can click on the number and type in whatever you want. In this case, we want **1**.

Figure 4.3   When TheButton is clicked, increase the value of its **Text** property by 1. This is incrementing the variable **TheButton.Text** on each click.

The **addition** block (+) adds the two numbers in its input sockets and then delivers the result to the left through its output socket. The two numbers we want to add are "whatever is currently in TheButton's Text" and 1. We use the getter **TheButton.Text** to retrieve the value of whatever is in that variable at that moment.

We then use the setter of **TheButton.Text** to take the result of the addition and store it back in the **Text** of TheButton. This set operation overwrites whatever is in there, so when we do this event again, we will get the new value from the getter block.

Now you have a Clicker-Counter app! Try it out. Every time you press the button, the number counts up by 1. It uses the Text **property** as a variable to hold whatever the current number is and then changes it, remembering the change. This is the basis of how all variables work: They store a value, which can be read with a getter and overwritten with something new with a setter.

Clicker Counter Extensions

Some extensions you could make to the Clicker-Counter app include the following:

- Add another button that resets the count to 0.
- Add another counter button that counts independently of the first.
- Change the counter to increase the value by 2 instead of 1 on each press.

Event Parameters: Special Variables

Think back to our first discussion on events. Everything in App Inventor is caused by an event. When a button is clicked, that is an event. When the phone is shaken, that is an event. When a text message arrives, that is an event. The events we've used so far have been pretty simple.

All you needed to know was that the event was happening. The button click is an instance of this: When the button is clicked, it runs the **Button.Click** event block and all the blocks in it. But not all events are so simple.

Some events provide extra information to you, the programmer, when they happen. In the following exercise, we talk about touching a canvas. A canvas is much more than a button. A canvas has a coordinate system, so when the user touches a canvas, you know that a touch happened, but you also know *where* it was touched. That *where* is extra information that needs to get into the event handler block to be used, and the way that information gets in is through event parameters. You can see them—they're the reddish rectangles in Figure 4.4 labeled *x* and *y*.

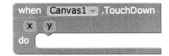

Figure 4.4   An event handler for touching down on a canvas, which also tells you the coordinate location of the touch in the *x* and *y* event parameters.

Every time this event happens, for each individual touch the user makes, this event runs and puts different information in those parameters. To get at this data, hover over their names with the mouse; a pop-up will appear with the getter block you need (see Figure 4.5). Grab the getter block out of the pop-up, and you can use that value.

Figure 4.5   Hover the mouse over the name of an event parameter, and a pop-up appears with the getter block.

You can also go into the Variables built-in menu and get a generic **get** block there. The **get** block, including the one you pulled out of the pop-up, has a pull-down menu (the little down arrow) that lets you change it to any variable that's currently available.

If you get a generic **get** block from the Variables menu, it won't show the event parameters in its pull-down menu until it is clicked into a block inside that event handler.

That brings us to our next point: Event parameters are valid only in that event. Having the *x* and *y* of the touch location elsewhere doesn't make sense: That information exists only when a **TouchDown** event occurs. You can certainly store it into another variable, but that event parameter itself works only inside the event it belongs to.

When you have a variable getter and it is detached from any blocks, it will likely have a red exclamation point on it, indicating an error (see Figure 4.6). If you click on it, it will tell you the error, which is probably "Select a valid item in the drop down." If you try to use the drop down, however, you'll find that it's empty. Don't worry—that drop down changes, depending on where you put the getter block. Connect it into an event with parameters, and those parameters instantly appear in the drop down. See Figure 4.7—the getter can see the event parameter variables because it is attached to that event.

Figure 4.6   A detached getter displays an error. Don't worry about it—that drop down will fill with choices based on the context where the block is attached.

Figure 4.7   Now attached, the getter can see the parameters for that event.

Exercise: Pollock

This next app gives you plenty of practice with event parameters. Better yet, it lets you and your users express some artistic freedom.

The end result is to create a drawing palette where the user will be able to create abstract art right on an Android phone. This app is loosely based on *Autumn Rhythm*, an abstract artwork by American artist Jackson Pollock (see Figure 4.8).

The Interface

1. To begin, create a new project and name it Pollock. Next, we will grab some elements in the Designer (these are laid out in Figure 4.9).

2. Drag a **HorizontalArrangement** component from the Layout drawer. This enables components to be put inside it, and they will be laid out from left to right.

3. From the User Interface, drag three buttons into the **HorizontalArrangement**. Rename each of them, calling them BrownButton, BlackButton, and WhiteButton, respectively.

Figure 4.8   The Pollock app (after some artistic expression by the user).

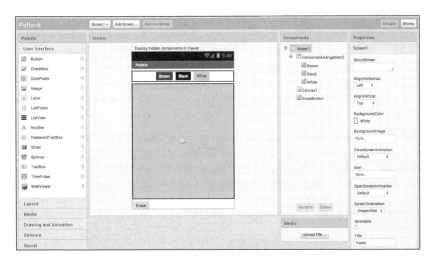

Figure 4.9   The Pollock app in the Designer.

4. When we add buttons in this area, centering them works better aesthetically. To do this, set the **HorizontalArrangement**'s width to Fill Parent and set its **AlignHorizontal** property to **Center**.

5. Now we want to change the color to match what we have named them. For each button, set its **BackgroundColor** property to the correct color that matches its name.

6. The button colors have been changed, but the text on the buttons does not yet display anything helpful. Type the appropriate color name into the **Text** property for each button.

7. We now need somewhere to draw. The canvas is just as it sounds, a platform we can draw colors on. Drag the canvas into the Viewer, and set the width to Fill Parent and the height to 340 pixels. This will fill the screen but leave enough room for the other elements we need.

8. Next, set the background color of the canvas to orange by selecting It from the **BackgroundColor** property near the top of the Properties box.

9. Don't be alarmed that the Erase button does not seem to fit in the Viewer. Odds are, it will appear just fine on most Android devices because the Viewer is only an approximation. We recommend always having a device connected with the companion app and checking how the app looks and performs as you go. *What shows up on the device is how the app really looks*, so design to that.

Programming Blocks

Now that we have the interface set, we need to program some blocks so the artistic creativity can take place.

1. In the drawer, click on **Canvas1** and pull out two different blocks: when **Canvas1.Touched** and when **Canvas1.Dragged** (see Figure 4.10).

   These blocks respond to two different actions that the user can take with the canvas. **Dragged** is triggered when the user slides a finger across the canvas. **Touched** is triggered when the user taps on the canvas in one place. In both of these events, we need to paint information about that specific drag or touch onto the canvas in the right place.

2. When the canvas is touched, we want to draw a circle where the person touched. From the canvas flyout menu, choose the **DrawCircle** procedure and click it into the **Touched** event. The **Touched** event provides the coordinates of where the touch took place. That is exactly where we want to draw our circle, so grab two getters (one for x, one for y) and attach them as shown in Figure 4.10. Also grab a number from the Math built-in menu and set it to 10 for the radius, or r, of the circle. You can ignore the **touchedSprite** parameter.

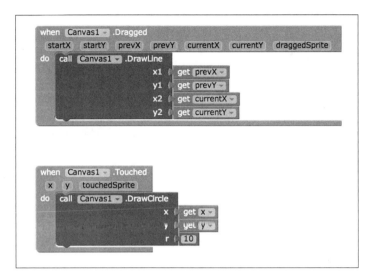

Figure 4.10   The blocks to handle canvas touch events.

3. When the user drags across the canvas, we want to draw a series of lines as he or she drags. The **Dragged** event offers three sets of coordinates. The ones we want for this are **prev** and **current.prev** always has the coordinate where the user's finger was last (as you drag), and **current** is where the user's finger now is. The **start** coordinates tell you where the user started the drag at the very beginning, but that's not important for drawing lines that follow the finger. We need to connect only the **prev** and **current** coordinates, and we will do it continually because this event runs repeatedly while the drag takes place. As you did earlier, find the **DrawLine** procedure from the canvas flyout menu and attach the blocks as shown in Figure 4.10.

4. We need three more event handler blocks to program the brown, black, and white color select buttons. The color select buttons change the color that is painted on the canvas (like a brush color). Each of these buttons has a **Click** event. Drag them all out. The canvas has a **PaintColor** property, which is what these buttons need to change. From the canvas flyout, choose the dark green setter for **Canvas.PaintColor** and duplicate it. (You can right-click and select Duplicate, or you can use Ctrl+C and Ctrl+V on the keyboard.) Put one in each of the color select button's click events. Then plug in the appropriate color for each one, as in Figure 4.11.

5. All that remains to set up is the Erase button. The Erase button will clear the palette when pressed. Choose the Erase button's Click event handler block. Insert the Clear procedure of the canvas into the **EraseButton.Click** event, as in Figure 4.11.

6. We have two different variable blocks for drawing, one for lines and the other for circles. The circles have a programmable radius, which we have currently set to 10. Try different values for the radius and see what size you prefer.

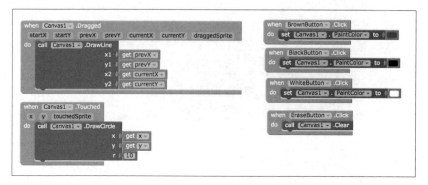

Figure 4.11   The blocks used in the Pollock app.

Test the app to make sure that it functions properly. This is another example that shows how important it is to have a device connected with the companion app while you work—you will be able to push and splatter the paint only on the phone. The emulator also works, but using the mouse just isn't the same as painting with your fingertips.

Additional Exercises

Some additional exercises you can try include the following:

1. The color scheme for this app was loosely based on Jackson Pollock's *Autumn Rhythm*. Try changing the color of the paint and the canvas for a different aesthetic.

2. The radius of **Circle** in the instructions was set to 10. Of course, you can change this. Right now, it's "hard-coded" with a number block. Expand the app so that users can change the radius as they paint. You'll need another component, and you need to have that component change a value that somehow will be hooked up to the radius. May I recommend a slider?

3. The canvas has other drawing features that we haven't used in this app. What else can you draw? Can you add features to the app to let the user do these things?

Scope: Global and Local Variables

So far in this chapter, we've used two kinds of variables that are built into existing parts of App Inventor: the properties of a component and the parameters to an event. You likely will soon encounter a case when you need your app to remember something but those two built-in variables won't do the job. You have two more kinds of variables available: global and local. In general, a variable is a location in the app that's invisible where you can store some information. All the variable types in this chapter have that in common: They hold data. They also have names that make it easy for humans to use them while working on the app.

A global variable is accessible anywhere in your blocks. It can be read or written to inside any block. It has global scope. Scope is the idea of where a variable is accessible or valid for use. The globe, in this case, is your whole blocks workspace. In contrast to the global variables, the event parameters are valid for use only inside their matching event handler. Their scope is limited to that event handler block.

All the component properties also have global scope. You can get a getter or setter block from the component's menu, and then you have no restrictions on where you can use it.

Global variables are used commonly in App Inventor. They can be used in the Clicker-Counter app, where a global variable holds the current number instead of the text of a button. That frees up the text of the button to display other data.

Global variables can hold data that doesn't change while the app runs, providing that data with a convenient name. In many cases, you simply want to name a value. In the Pollock app, we explicitly set the radius to 10 using a number block. We can easily make a global variable to hold that. If we name it something like **dot_radius** and set the value in it to **10**, we could hook up the dot_radius getter to the *r* input of the **DrawCircle** procedure, as in Figure 4.12.

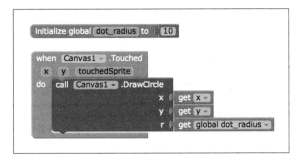

Figure 4.12   Replacing the hard-coded *r* with a global variable that has a nice name.

Now that we have a nice name, looking at that DrawCircle block is a little easier. The inputs all have names that explain them, including *r*. If we want to change the radius, we could change the initialization and restart the app. Or we could use an orange setter block to change it in the code so that it can change while the app is being used, maybe in response to the user's desires. The variable holding the value makes that possible.

App Inventor has one more kind of variable: the local variable. As you might guess, *local* describes the scope of the variable. Unlike the global, the local is valid only in a certain place in your code. This is similar to the event parameter, but you get to set up a local variable wherever you need it. You can create and use local variables from the Variables built-in menu, shown in Figure 4.13. Both global and local variables are discussed in more detail later in this chapter.

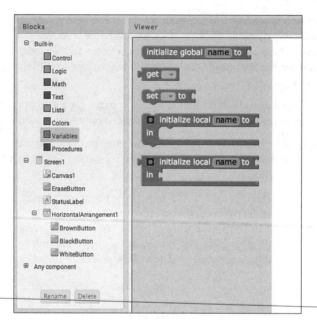

Figure 4.13   The Variables built-in menu.

Global Variables

Global variables need to be initialized before they can be used. The **initialize global** block does three things: creates the variable, gives it a name, and sets its initial value.

Choose the **initialize** block from the Variables built-in menu, and then click in the Name field to replace the word name with a useful name. The **initialize** block *must* have an initial value. This is similar to setting a value of a component property in the Designer; you have to put in *something* for the app to have in that variable when it starts. A variable cannot be truly empty.

Usually, the value given to the **initialize** block is useful and relevant, such as setting a counter variable to start at zero. Sometimes you just need space for later and you need to have some value to get the variable initialized. In these cases, you can give it a number zero, or an empty text block, or an empty list block, but you need to give it something for the variable to exist.

What is initialization? A variable needs to be created before it is used. This happens in one of the early moments during the app's startup. After that, you can change the value using the setter block.

When you create a global variable, you can access it anywhere in your blocks, allowing that variable to be shared among blocks. We covered that earlier. But one more property of global variables makes them useful: That value is changeable anywhere and readable anywhere, but there is still just one value. You can use global variables to keep parts of your app synchronized, such as keeping a label and a picture in sync as your user pages through a slide show. The variable still is just one storage box, regardless of how many parts of your app are using it. One event might change the variable, and then when any other event looks at the value, it instantly gets the updated value.

Example App: Up/Down Counter

This app is the same basic idea as the Clicker-Counter app from earlier in the chapter, but with some differences:

- The current count will be displayed in a label.
- The current count will be stored in a global variable.
- Two buttons will be used: one to increase count and one to decrease it.

You can set it up something like Figure 4.14, with a label and two buttons.

Figure 4.14   The Up/Down Counter app, in the Designer.

The programming of this app is also simple. Whenever the number is changed by the up or down button, two things need to happen: update the variable with a new value and display that new value in the label.

In both click events for both buttons, the variable count changes and the text of the label updates, as in Figure 4.15. The variable always holds the current count. Other things could be added that would change the label text, and the count could be preserved in the variable. The global variable exists as exactly one storage location but is accessible anywhere in the blocks.

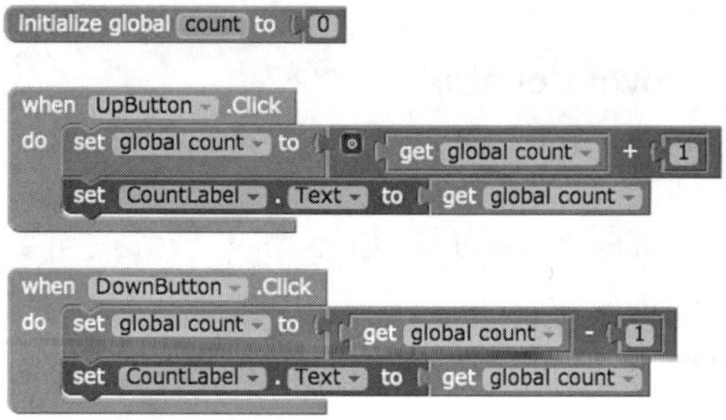

Figure 4.15   The blocks for the Up/Down Counter app, using the variable **count** to store the current value.

You will see another great example of using a variable to keep track of things when we get to lists in Chapter 6, "Working with Lists." We'll actually use them throughout the book, and you'll likely use them throughout your app making.

Local Variables

The last type of variable is the local. It is a variable, so we know that it is a storage location with a name where we can put values in and read them out. A local variable needs to be explicitly initialized, like a global, and uses orange getters and setters, also like a global. What makes this one different is that the scope of the variable is limited. You can actually control exactly what the scope is, and that's both cool and useful. Take a look at a local variable block in Figure 4.16. Note the notches on the top and bottom. Those mean that it clicks into a stack of action blocks: setters, procedure calls, and so on. It also has the same notch inside it, where you can put more action blocks. In addition, you can see an input socket where you put the initialization value.

Figure 4.16   A local variable block.

Here's where the local gets interesting. That variable, which you can rename to anything you want (it's still **name** in Figure 4.16), exists only within that C-shaped block. If you read the block's text, it forms a sentence: "Initialize local (some name) to (some value) in (some blocks)." Whatever blocks you put in the "some blocks" section will be able to see and use the variable. When those blocks finish running and App Inventor gets to the bottom of the local block, the local ceases to exist; the rest of the code stack below it (if there is any) then runs without any knowledge of that variable ever having happened.

Take a look at Figure 4.17. This is a valid use of a local variable. When BigButton is clicked, it creates a new variable *at that time* called **temp_value** and initializes it to that text. When we go to set the status label's text, we can use that variable to get at the text in it. After the label is set, we get to the end of the local block, so the local disappears; any subsequent blocks won't be able to set it or read it.

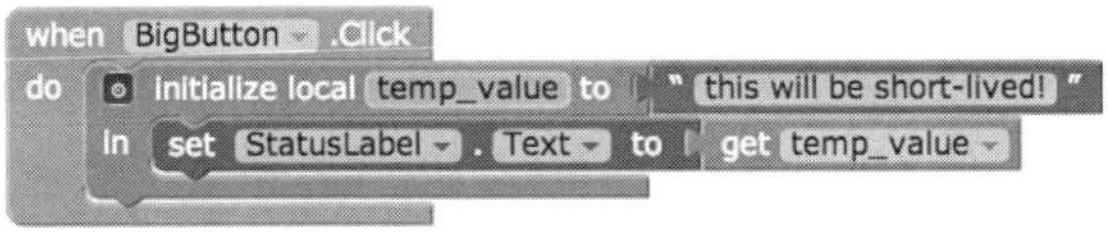

Figure 4.17   A simple use of a local variable. That variable will exist only inside the red block.

Now look at Figure 4.18. It's the same as Figure 4.17, but it has an invalid attempt to see the local variable outside its scope. Outside that red local block, the variable doesn't exist, so it can't be accessed. App Inventor immediately detects that the variable isn't in scope, so it puts a red error indicator on the block. If you look at the pull-down menu for that get block, you won't find **temp_value**. You will find any globals that exist, but until that getter is back inside the red local block, the local can't be used or seen by it.

Figure 4.18   The getter for the local variable is outside the variable's scope, so it doesn't work. The red exclamation point indicates the error. This figure is doing it wrong!

An Example App: Random Guess

Pick a number from 1 to 10. Now have your opponent try to guess that number. Don't give any hints; just say whether the guess is right or wrong. Imagine that your opponent is the computer, and it's guessing at total random. That's the app we're going to build.

The interface is really simple, as in Figure 4.19. You can elaborate on the design, but for now, let's just get to the good stuff: the local variable. Use a button to get the computer to make a guess. Two labels will tell the user what the latest computer guess was and whether it was correct.

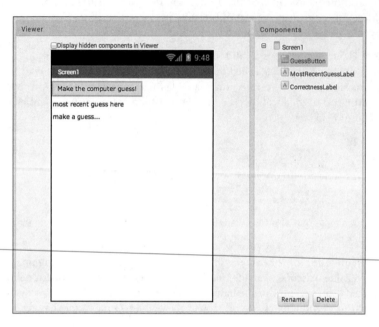

Figure 4.19   The Random Guess app in the Designer.

Figure 4.20 shows the blocks for this app. The first thing you likely see is a global variable called **target**. This is the number the computer is trying to guess. For now, we'll hard-code it to 5. You can change it or make a way for the user to change it.

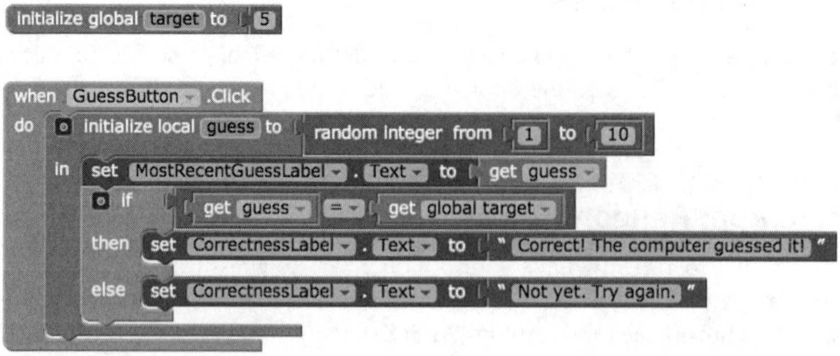

Figure 4.20   The blocks for the Random Guess app. Note the use of the local variable to temporarily hold the random guess.

When the GuessButton is clicked, a local variable named guess is created; then it is initialized to a random number from 1 to 10.

Inside the local variable block, a label's text is updated to show the user what the guess is. Then an **if** block asks the question, "Is the guess equal to the target value?" If the answer is yes, the CorrectnessLabel text says so, printing "Correct!" on the screen. If not, that label is updated to read "Not yet. Try again."

Here's why the local variable is important for this app to work. Every time you use the random integer block, you get a new random number. We want to make one random number and then use it twice. See how the **get guess** block is used more than once? If we just asked for a random integer more than once, each of those would be different, and the app wouldn't behave properly.

We are using the local variable to capture one random value into the variable named **guess**, and then when this click event is over and the all the work is done, it will be forgotten. There's no need to clutter up the world with a global variable when we need to remember the value for only a short span of blocks.

After pressing the Guess button some number of times (possibly around 10?), the computer will stumble randomly onto the right answer. This is the case in Figure 4.21, which shows the app running.

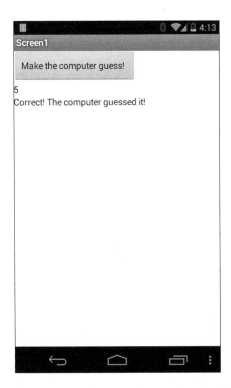

Figure 4.21   The Random Guess app running on a phone. The computer guessed the number!

What You Can Store in Variables

In this chapter, we've dealt mostly with storing number values in variables. This section is here to clarify that you can store *any* kind of value in variables. Figure 4.22 shows a few of the various types that can be stored in variables.

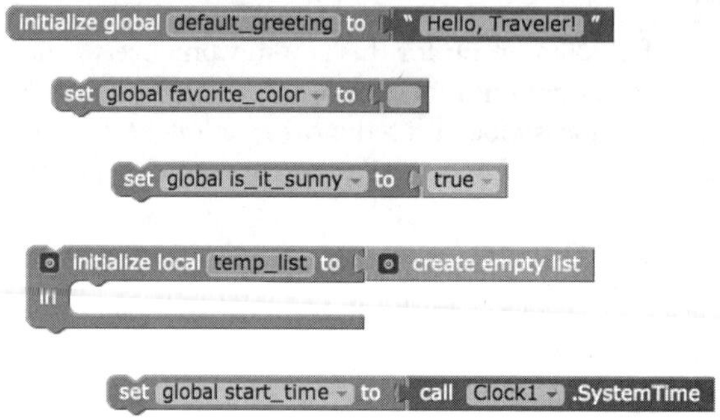

Figure 4.22   A few examples of what you can store in variables.

No limitations restrict the types you can store in global or local variables. Any block that has a left-pointing socket can be stored in these variables.

Component properties, which we used like variables, are built into the components to provide certain functions, so whatever you store in them has to make sense for what they're used for. If you tried to store the text **hello** in the component property **TextBox.Width**, it wouldn't make sense. The component needs that property to be a number because it's a measurement of width in pixels, and random text isn't going to satisfy it.

The App Inventor system uses event parameters to give you information so you should only have to read them, never set them. With this, you don't have to worry about types; all parameters do is hand you data that's ready to go.

Global variables, like component properties, are initialized early in the app's startup process. That means that they can be initialized to only "known" things, like hard-coded values (such as **5** or **hello**). The app is not fully running yet when the globals are initialized, so you can't set their starting values to anything that depends on code running (pick a random number) or other components existing (text in a text box).

Summary

Component properties are variables that are built into a component. Setting a component property's value in the Designer sets the starting value of that property. It can be changed as the app runs—by blocks, by the user, or both. Component properties are accessible with the green getter and setter blocks for that component, and they have global scope.

Event parameters are special variables that give you extra information about an event. Event parameter variables are valid only inside the event handler they belong to (meaning that they have limited scope). Each time the event runs, you might get different information in those parameters, which reflects the details of that one occurrence of the event. Event parameters use the orange getter block.

Global variables have global scope, meaning that they can be set and read from any blocks in the workspace (which is the "globe" your blocks live in). You can store any value in global variables. Globals must be initialized to a value with an initialization block and then can be read and changed with the orange getter and setter blocks, respectively. Global variables appear only in the code blocks; they can't be seen in the Designer, and the user can't directly see them.

Local variables work like global variables: They can store any value, they must be initialized to a value, and they can be accessed with the orange getter and setter. Local variables have local scope, meaning that they exist only within their initialization block, which has space to add more blocks. Outside that block, a local variable no longer exists. A local is reinitialized every time its initialization block runs. Locals, like globals, are also accessible only directly in the blocks.

Component properties and global variables are initialized to their starting values when the app first starts up, before the app is fully running. Their start values must not depend on code running or components existing. They should always be hard-coded values. Local variables are initialized on demand while the app is fully running, whenever their block is encountered, so they don't have this restriction.

5

Procedures

Apps can perform many different tasks. The more complex the application, the more programming is required to make these specific tasks happen. As you build more utility into your App Inventor apps, the number of blocks can get rather unruly. By learning to use procedures, you can keep your code nice and tidy while building in all the specific instructions necessary for each app.

The following section gives you a more detailed description of how procedures work in the App Inventor. Then we practice using some procedures before putting them to use in the exercise at the end of the chapter.

This exercise gives you some good practice, but it should be the start of applying procedures to apps in different circumstances. Procedures are a key part of many types of apps, so mastering this skill will be extremely useful.

What Is a Procedure?

A procedure is a set of instructions that is grouped together, given a name, and made available for later use. This makes your code easier to read, think about, and change. Ultimately, using a procedure is more powerful. The steps for getting started are fairly straightforward.

Adding a procedure is accomplished through a simple command in the Blocks Editor (see Figure 5.1).

Procedures dramatically improve the process of building multistep features into your app. Often an app needs to perform the same action several times or in different circumstances. Creating a procedure enables you to quickly add this action to your app without needing to reconstruct or copy and paste the code every time. Plus, copied code makes it harder to fix your app when you troubleshoot issues. If something needs to change in the original version of your app, you then need to find all the copies and make the same change over and over. By using a procedure, you need to make only a single change.

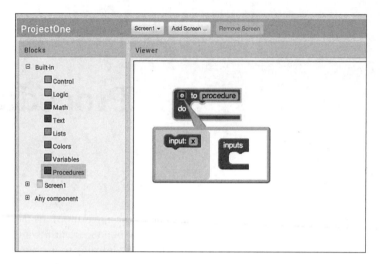

Figure 5.1   Adding a procedure in the Blocks Editor.

Additionally, you can use procedures to give any sequence of blocks a name. When a collection of blocks has a name, you don't have to worry about how it works—you can just pick it out of the menu as a single block and use it.

Types of Procedures

The Procedures drawer has two Procedures blocks: **do** and **result**. You can find them by clicking the Procedures block in the drawer (see Figure 5.2).

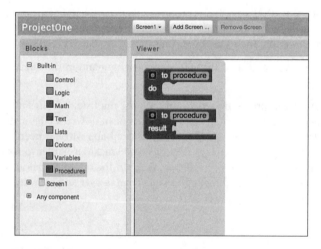

Figure 5.2   The **do** and **result** procedures.

The **do** procedure collects a sequence of blocks into one group. This same collection of blocks can then be called later, which means the blocks in this **do** group will be run in order every time you use the procedure. When you give the set of blocks a custom name, that set appears below the **do** and **result** options in the drawer.

The **result** block has a differently shaped slot. This kind of procedure provides a result value when it is done. When this procedure is called, it runs the blocks in the procedure, and whatever value ends up at that result socket is returned, sort of like a variable getter. To best understand this, let's look at the new blocks that get created as a result of defining procedures.

After you use a **do** block to define a procedure, a new block appears in the Procedures menu (see Figure 5.3).

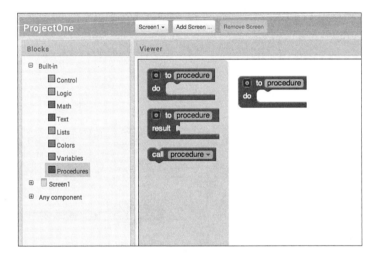

Figure 5.3   Using a **do** block creates another new block in the Procedures menu.

The new block, **call**, shares its name with the procedure you just defined. In Figure 5.3, the procedure doesn't have any blocks in the definition, so when it is called, it won't do anything. Let's add something to the definition (see Figure 5.4).

You can drag out the **update text call** block and use it anywhere in your app. Whenever that block is run, it runs whatever is in the definition (in this example, this is to set the text of TextBox1 to be "New Message!").

Using the result definition works a little differently: It gives you a **call** block that returns a result value (see Figure 5.5).

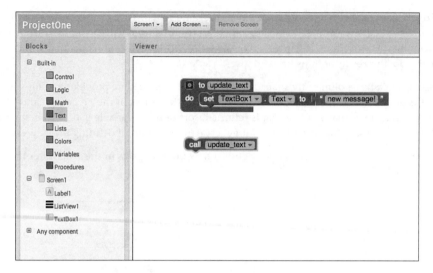

Figure 5.4   Programming a message.

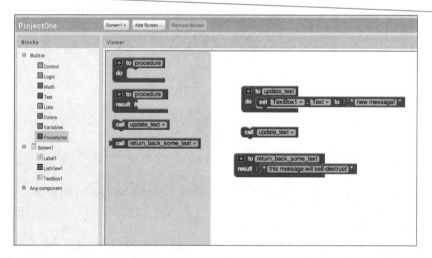

Figure 5.5   Using the result definition.

When called, the procedure named **return_some_text** runs the blocks in its definition—in this example, it simply produces a piece of text and returns that out of the socket on the left side of the **call** block. That **call** block can be hooked up to any input socket of any other block. This is useful for hiding complex operations, such as arithmetic or text processing, behind a simple procedure name.

Why Use Procedures?

Using procedures to name sequences of code gives you two advantages:

- You can hide the work required to perform a task, which could be big and complicated, behind a single block that has a descriptive name.

- You can reduce duplicate code, which makes your app easier to debug, update, and read. Having an excessive number of duplicated blocks can make debugging or changing an app needlessly difficult.

When creating a procedure, it is always a good idea to assign it a descriptive name. This adds meaning and makes it easier for you to recall this specific procedure later (refer to Figure 5.5). To change the name of the procedure, click in the oval after **procedure** and then type in a different name. Each procedure name must be unique (which is a good practice anyway when naming components or other items).

After you rename the procedure, a new choice appears in the blocks drawer. As Figure 5.5 shows, a new, named procedure is now available for use.

Arguments

An argument is a way to give information to a procedure when it is called. You already provided arguments to procedures when you used a block with an open socket(s), such as when you set the value in a textbox. The value you connect to the **set** block is an argument. Creating a procedure with an argument involves the mutator, which is the small blue box with a white gear. Clicking this blue icon enables you to drag additional smaller blocks onto the larger block.

With procedures, the little blocks in the mutator add arguments. Each argument is a named value of information that will be passed into the procedure whenever it is called. These values are inputs to the procedure. This changes the shape of the call block, adding sockets for you to supply those input values.

In Figure 5.6, we have a complex formula. We're using this sequence of blocks to convert a number from an accelerometer reading to a screen position. By using the **do** block, you can create another block that responds to the equation.

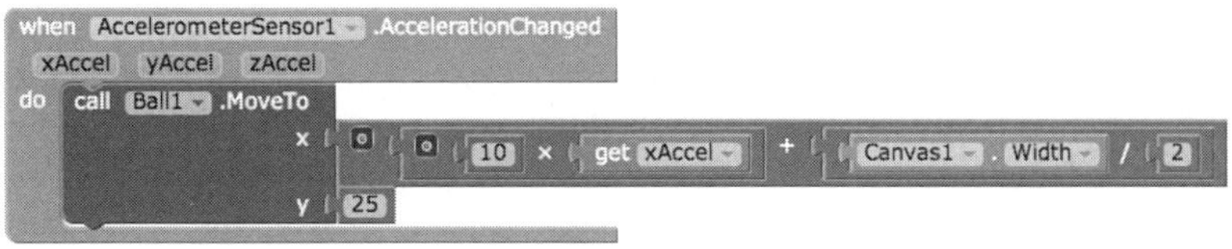

Figure 5.6   Using a **do** block creates another block in the Procedures menu.

That chunk of arithmetic blocks is important, but we don't need to look at these blocks all the time for them to do their job. If we create a procedure, we can hide the arithmetic behind a simple name. The purpose of the blocks is to scale a value, so we'll create a new procedure named **scale_reading** (see Figure 5.7). The mutator adds an input to the procedure definition. The name of the input changes to **accel_reading**, to give it a descriptive name.

Figure 5.7   The new procedure is called **scale_reading**.

Now that we have a procedure defined that handles the math, we can call that procedure in our existing code, replacing the messy arithmetic with a single block (see Figure 5.8).

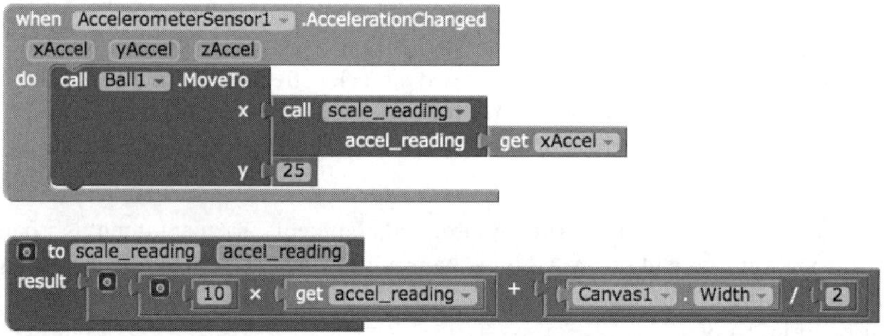

Figure 5.8   The new procedure replaces the messy arithmetic.

The best part of this new procedure is how easy it is to read the **AccelerationChanged** code. Before, we saw a big cluster of blocks, and figuring out what those blocks did was tricky. Now there's an easier sentence to read, with the complicated part replaced by the procedure scale reading. So whatever is going into the right side of that procedure block is a reading, which is being scaled; then that result comes out the left side. This makes it easier to focus on what the remaining code is doing with the value returned from the procedure without regard to how that value was calculated.

If you want to know the details of how the scaling works, or if you want to change those details, look at the definition. Any change to the definition instantly changes how the call works.

Exercise: Flick

The app Flick (see Figure 5.9) creates a ball that can be flicked across the screen or moved by shaking the phone.

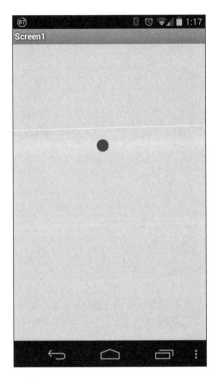

Figure 5.9   The final product of the app.

1. To begin, open a new project and name it Flick.

2. Drag out a canvas. We then want it to fill the screen, so change the width and height on the canvas to Fill Parent. This tells the canvas to take up all the available space in the app.

3. Drag out a ball. Drop it into the canvas; ball components can be placed only in a canvas. To make it a little easier to see and flick, change the size by making the Radius 10 (see Figure 5.10).

4. We currently have a black ball on a white canvas. Let's add a little color to the mix. Select the canvas from the components and change the background color to green. Then click on the ball and change the paint color to blue.

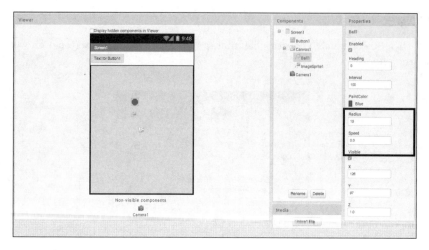

Figure 5.10   The Radius adjusts the speed of the ball.

5. Switch to the Blocks Editor and pull out the Flung event handler for the **Ball1** block (see Figure 5.11). The Flung event is called when the user "flings" a ball or Image Sprite component. After the ball has been flung, we need to set a speed and direction of movement for the ball (see Figure 5.11).

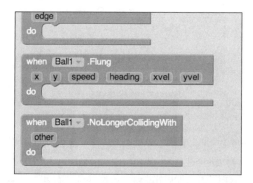

Figure 5.11   Grabbing this block tells the ball what to do when flung.

6. We next need two commands from the same location; grab the **set Ball1 speed** and **set Ball1 Heading** blocks and place them inside the **Ball.Flung** event handler.

7. We now need information provided to us from the Android device. To access the speed of the fling, hover the mouse (don't click) over the orange speed variable. To access the speed, grab the **get speed** block and connect it to the **set Ball Speed** block. To move the ball in the direction of the fling, repeat the process, connecting the **get heading** block to the **set ball heading** block (see Figure 5.12).

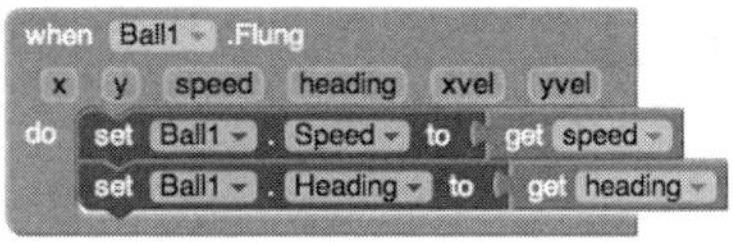

Figure 5.12   The blocks should appear like this.

8. We now have the ball that will move around the screen when flicked. The harder you flick, the farther and faster the ball will travel. However, when it hits the wall, it will stick to it. Fortunately, Android has provided a means of determining such an occurrence. Android will call the **EdgeReached** event when a ball or Image Sprite touches the edge of the canvas.

9. To have the ball rebound when it touches the edge, grab the **when Ball1 EdgeReached** event handler block. Drop into this event handler the **Ball1.Bounce** command. This command tells the ball to change directions. If we tell the **Bounce** command what edge was touched, it will know the appropriate changes to make in the direction the ball is traveling. We do this by hovering over the orange edge variable and connecting its **get** block to the **Bounce** command (see Figure 5.13).

Figure 5.13   The ball will now bounce off the edges.

10. Try the app again—the ball should now flick across the screen and bounce off the walls.

Additional Exercises

1. Change the speed of the ball so that it slows down and stops after it is flung. Experiment with different speeds and see which is optimal for how you would like the app to function.

2. Change the color and size of the ball and the canvas, seeing how different iterations look (see Figure 5.14). Use this as an opportunity to see how these changes impact both the look and the functionality of the app.

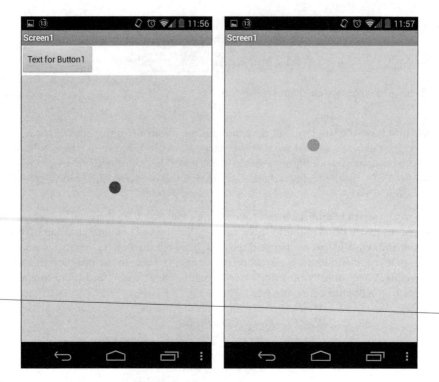

Figure 5.14   Different colors and sizes of the canvas.

Summary

Creating and using procedures helps make more consistent and easier-to-follow code. As you saw in this application, you can reduce the amount of programming time by calling blocks of code.

As we build more complex apps, using procedures will make the workload more manageable and support applications that are easier to tweak, debug, and customize. As you learn to build lists, work with sensors, and manage GPS coordinates, you will find that the block code can get rather large. Using procedures is a way to make this more controlled and give you the ability to more quickly go back into the blocks to see if you need to resolve any issues.

Procedures will continue to play a role in other applications you build—also be on the lookout for how the apps you use were probably made possible by creating some kind of procedure.

Working with Lists

Lists are a way to organize and work with data. Learning to effectively use lists is one of the most important tasks in building good apps with App Inventor.

Lists serve an important purpose in general programming as well. Consider how a news app has lists of sections. Think about how a social network, such as Google+, has lists of a user's friends. App Inventor has an easy-to-learn but powerful method for implementing lists into mobile apps. Any collection of data can be represented as a list or as multiple lists working together.

Modeling Things with Data

Lists are a method for organizing sets of data. You might write that data right into the blocks of the app, and it will never change. Alternatively, the user might input that data while the app is running. That data might even be a series of sensor readings, such as those from the GPS, or a list of restaurants the app pulled from the Internet. Data can take many forms, whether a list of contacts, a collection of GPS coordinates, or a bank of questions (we use the latter with the Android Quiz app later in this chapter).

Good use of data requires not just getting it, but also learning how it can tell a story or be part of a larger purpose. Next, we look at how MIT App Inventor specifically can empower you to do this.

The List Block

In App Inventor, we will be using the blocks in the Lists menu (see Figure 6.1). For reference, an entire list of the different list blocks is located on the App Inventor support site.

You can expand or shrink some of the list blocks by clicking the gear in the upper-left corner (refer to Figure 6.1). This enables you to add smaller blocks to the larger block (see Figure 6.2).

Figure 6.1   The list blocks.

Figure 6.2   The **make a list** block, with the item-adding menu (called a mutator) open.

For example, consider the **make a list** block. To add items to this block, click the blue gear button in the top left. A pop-out window then displays a sublist of items that you can drag into and out of the main list block (see Figure 6.2).

Doing this changes that **make a list** block to have the same number of inputs as the **number of item** blocks you dragged in from the pop-out. This pop-out window, and the gear button it hides behind, is called a *mutator* because it can mutate, or change, the block you're using. Many other blocks in App Inventor also have mutators, and they all have one thing in common: They adapt the block to fit the kind of input you want to give it.

With the **make a list** block, after you've selected how many items you want in it, it will accept that many inputs. Inputs can be any data value: a number, a color, text, or even another list. The **make a list** block will return, through its output socket, a new list that contains all the items you gave it, in order.

Don't worry: You'll be able to modify the list as the app runs—or maybe you don't need to. It all depends on what you want your app to do. App Inventor's list features are powerful and let you do whatever you need.

The Basics

A list is multiple pieces of data stuck together, one after another. Those pieces of data are in order, meaning that whatever is in slot 1 of the list will stay there unless you move it. Every item in the list has a number, starting with 1. Figure 6.3 shows what lists look like to the phone. Each cell is a place you can put something (a number, a piece of text, or anything else), and each something has a number. There are no empty items: Each item has to have *something* in it, and no numbers are skipped.

The list itself is a container. Regardless of how much stuff is inside it, it can be treated, as a whole, as a single piece of data. Lists can be stored in variables (they are just a type of data) and passed as inputs and outputs to blocks. Let's go over all these features.

Figure 6.3   What a list looks like in the phone's memory.

Creating an Empty List

For now, we're going to make some lists and store them in variables. This is a common technique, but keep in mind that lists don't *always* have to go straight into variables.

To create our first list, we're going to create a global variable definition (refer to Chapter 4, "Variables") and drag in the **create empty list** block (see Figure 6.4).

Figure 6.4   Create a global variable definition and drag in the **create empty list** block.

Now we have a list! We can give it a name by renaming the global variable. Let's call it **my_list** (see Figure 6.5).

Figure 6.5   Rename the global variable to **my_list**.

Now whenever you use the getter block for that variable (**my_list**), you'll get a list and whatever is in that list at the time (see Figure 6.6).

get global my_list ▾

Figure 6.6   The getter block for the global variable named **my_list**, which contains a list.

Right now, the list is empty, which is perfectly valid. This list simply has zero items in it—you can add things to it later.

Creating a List with Some Stuff Already In It

Now we're going to create a list in a different way. We're still going to initialize a global variable, but we're going to use the **make a list** block, which takes inputs. You can change how many items the **make a list** block will accept (how many input sockets it has) by clicking the gear and dragging items into and out of the mutator that pops up (see Figure 6.7).

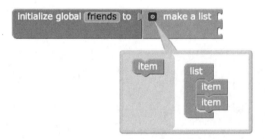

Figure 6.7   Drag items into the mutator until you have the number of list items you need.

Add one more item to the list block so that it has three inputs. Then we'll give it three pieces of data, which will be in the list right away when the app starts up. Why do you get the items right away? Because they're part of the global variable initialization that happens when the app starts. Not all data is available at app startup, but we'll deal with that later in the chapter.

We added three names to the definition of the list and renamed the global variable to **friends**. Look at Figure 6.8—it's a list of friends!

Figure 6.8   A list of friends.

Now we'll talk about things we can do with lists.

The ListPicker

One easy thing we can do is give the user a way to select an item in a list, using a ListPicker component (see Figure 6.9). ListPickers look like buttons, as in Figure 6.10, but when pressed, they open a full-screen list view in which users can pick any item they like.

Figure 6.9   The ListPicker icon in the Designer palette.

Figure 6.10   The ListPicker looks like a button in the app.

To make the ListPicker work, we must tell it what we want the selectable items to be. This information is stored in the **Elements** property of the ListPicker, so we'll have to set that. We want to show our friends list, so we'll set the ListPicker's elements to be our global variable **friends**, as in Figure 6.11. Now we know how to set the elements—we just need to know when to do so.

set ListPicker1 . Elements to get global friends

Figure 6.11   How to set the elements of the ListPicker to an existing list (but one that's not finished yet).

The ListPicker has an event named **BeforePicking**, which is run the moment the user clicks the button but before the ListPicker appears in full screen. We can use this moment to set up the ListPicker. We'll use that to tell it which list to show (see Figure 6.12).

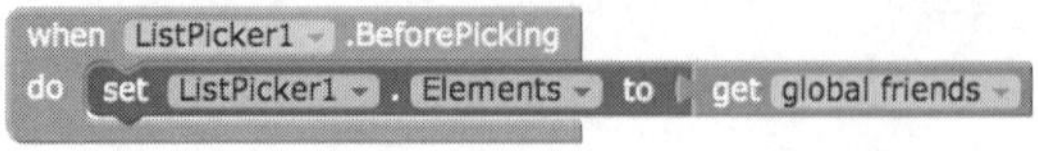

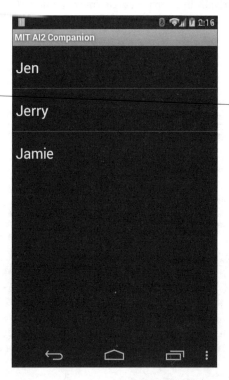

Figure 6.12   Update the elements in the **BeforePicking** event.

Let's give it a try. Press the ListPicker button; it will populate its Elements from the list of friends we gave it, and the three names will appear. It should look something like Figure 6.13.

Figure 6.13   A pickable list!

You (or your user) can select any of these three; the ListPicker then closes. We haven't told it what to do with this selection, so it doesn't do anything with it yet. Let's do one more thing, just for fun: Let's update the text of the ListPicker (the part that looks like a button) to reflect the selection that was picked. It's easy. The ListPicker stores whatever the user picked in a property called **selection**. We want to set the text of the ListPicker to the Selection, and we want to do it after the user picks something. Conveniently, there's an event for that: **AfterPicking**. Put it all together, as in Figure 6.14, and the button changes to match your selection. (The button will change to look like Figure 6.15.)

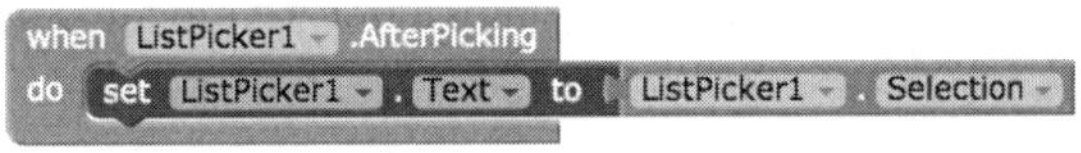

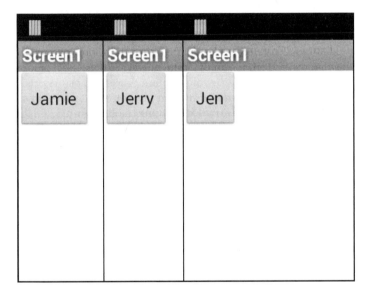

Figure 6.14   Updating the text to match whatever the user picked.

Figure 6.15   Whatever you pick, it appears!

Working with Lists

When you have a list (it can be empty, too), you can do something with it. For starters, you can add a new item to the end of the list. If the list had n items before, then after you add the new one, it will have $n+1$ items; the last item will be item number $n+1$. This is done with the block **add items to list**.

You can get the number of items in the list using the **length of list** block. It's often useful to know how long a list is so you don't try to ask for data that's not there. If you ever ask for an item that doesn't exist, the app will create an error, which the user will see. For example, if a list has five items and you try to get item number 6 (or higher), that item doesn't exist and thus will trigger an error. Try not to let this happen.

Take a look at the Lists palette flyout (refer to Figure 6.1), and check out the various other operations you have available. We will exercise a few more as we learn about lists themselves.

Lists are very powerful and expressive, and they serve many uses when programming.

Color as a List

You might have noticed the built-in blocks palette called Colors. In it are 13 color blocks, which make setting the colors of background and buttons in code blocks quick and easy. But the really interesting part is at the bottom of the palette: the **make color** block (see Figure 6.16).

Figure 6.16   Making a custom color out of a list. This one has red at maximum and blue and green at zero. The color will be red.

Colors in App Inventor are really just lists. These lists must have exactly three items in them, and those items must be numbers, which specify the red, green, and blue parts of the color. Using the **make color** block, you can create whatever color you like, and properties such as **BackgroundColor** will accept it. This can allow you to create any color in the RGB rainbow. *One note:* The numeric values must be between 0 and 255 for each element.

The take-away here is that colors are just lists of numbers describing red, green, and blue. You can create a new color from a list, or take an existing color and turn it back into a list (using the **split color** block).

Types of Lists

You have learned the basics of lists. Now let's look more systematically at the different kinds of lists in MIT App Inventor.

The One-Dimensional List

A single list is a one-dimensional structure. This is just like any list you would write on paper. It has items in an order from top to bottom (or left to right, depending on how you want to think about it). If we have a list, we can add things to it, whenever we want, nearly forever.

Here are some code blocks that will take the text from a text box and add it to a list every time a button is pressed (see Figure 6.17). This could be the beginnings of a note-taking app or a reminder app. The user types something in, and that is added to the list inside the phone when the button is pressed.

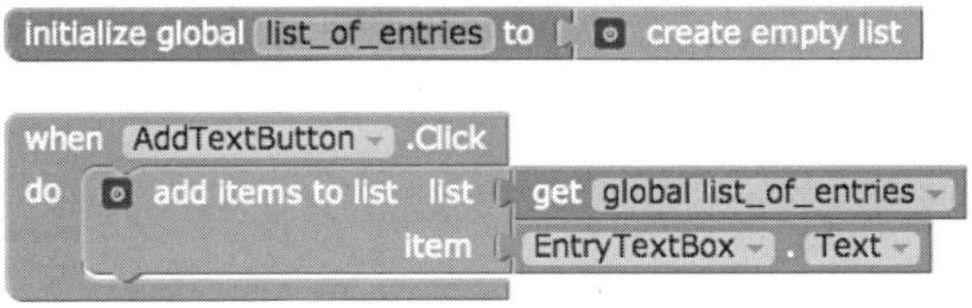

Figure 6.17   A copy of the text box text is added to the list every time the button is clicked.

This list will grow every time the button is clicked.

Lists as Data Structures

Sometimes you don't need a long, expanding list of entries. Sometimes you have just a few things that you want to keep organized and together. You can use lists to create little structures for your things, much like the color list gave structure to red, green, and blue values.

For instance, consider an app that keeps track of bills that need to be paid each month. For each bill, the user inputs a name (text), a day of the month it is due (number), and an amount (number). We can use a list to bind these three things together into a single unit that we can move around. Figure 6.18 shows such a list, which we can then consider to be "a bill."

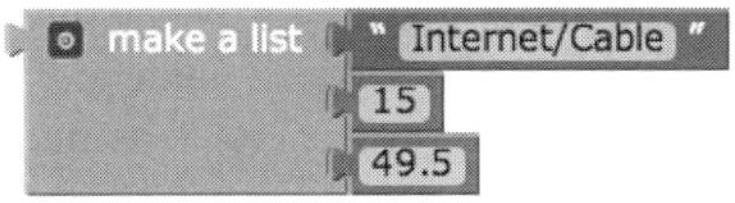

Figure 6.18   A list that provides structure for "a bill," made from a name, a due day, and a cost.

This small list shows us a few things. First, lists can have different kinds of data in them. A single list can have one item that is text, another that is a number, or any other value in App Inventor. Lists are heterogeneous, which makes structures such as our bill info possible.

So what do we do with this list structure now that we have it? Whatever we need. We know that we can pass around a single item (the list), and inside that list we have declared that the first item will always be the name, the second item will always be the due date, and the third item will always be the price. If we have three labels onscreen that we want to use to display a bill's information, we can take apart our structure to fill them. The blocks in Figure 6.19 do just that, assuming that there is a bill structure stored in the global variable **bill1**. Note how they are all using the same input, the bill structure, and just taking out the parts that they need.

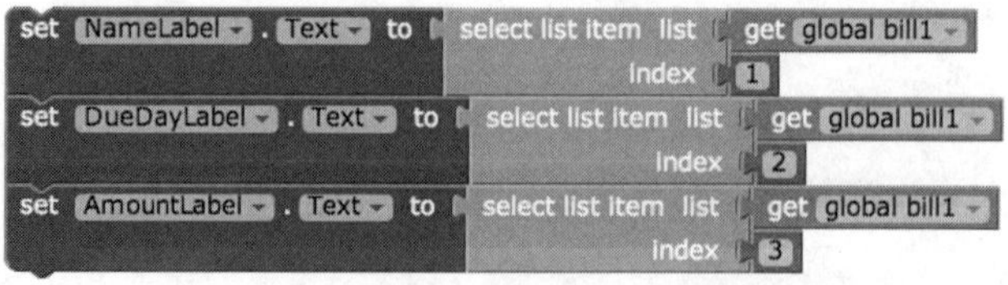

Figure 6.19   Taking apart the bill structure to set appropriate labels.

We have seen two different examples of lists as data structures: one with color and one with a bill. In both cases, we can consider the list to be a single object, an *abstraction* of the thing we are representing. We can think about the color red, but really, it's just a list of **255**, **0**, and **0**. But we don't need to think about the details—we have to worry about only the final product. The same goes for the bill abstraction: When we have our list with three pieces, we can treat that list as a single bill and worry about the details some other time. This is a powerful idea in computing: We can make it so that we have to worry about only certain details at a time. It makes thinking and reasoning with complex systems easier for our human brains.

One more data structure example remains: a name and number for an address book. We'll look at this in the next section.

Using Multiple Lists Together (That Expand on Demand)

An alternative to using small lists as structures is to use multiple lists, with each list holding a piece of the data.

Let's design one more data structure out of a list: a phone book contact entry. Our contacts app will be very simple. Each entry will contain a person's name and phone number. We will need two lists for this (one to hold the names and one to hold the numbers), and they will work together to keep the information organized.

This example works much like the one in Figure 6.17, where we added a new item each time a button was clicked. In this case, when a button is clicked, we're going to take two pieces of information, the name and number, from the user via two text boxes and put them into their respective lists. The code to that is fairly simple, as you can see in Figure 6.20.

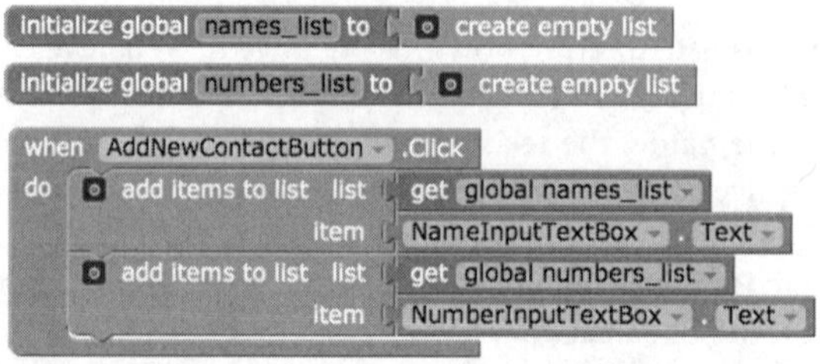

Figure 6.20   Adding new contact data to two lists, one for names, one for numbers.

Now that we have the data, using two lists, we need to be able to put the lists together to see our data. The lists relate by index, meaning that item 1 in the **names_list** belongs to item 1 in the **numbers_list**. This is true for any item. Item *n* in the **names_list** will be the name that belongs to the number in position *n* in the **numbers_list**. This is the key point of this technique: The list indices match up. We know that they match up because we added both at the same time in Figure 6.20.

Figure 6.21 is a screenshot of a possible contacts app. The name and number input text boxes are the ones in Figure 6.20, which add the contact information to our lists. The Display Contacts button then uses that data to fill in a label, with one line per item. The key to making this work is the **for each number** loop, in Figure 6.22. This loop repeats a set of actions over and over again, counting up a variable (number) with each repetition. It takes three inputs: the "from" number, or where it starts counting; the "to" number, or where it stops counting; and the "by" number, or by how much it increases on each repetition. We'll leave "by" at 1 because we want to count by 1. We'll also leave "from" at 1 because we want to start with the first item in our lists.

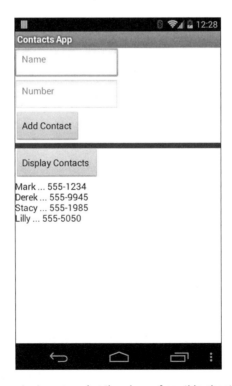

Figure 6.21   A possible contacts app, using the pieces from this chapter. (The blue bar is just a label stretched out with a background color.)

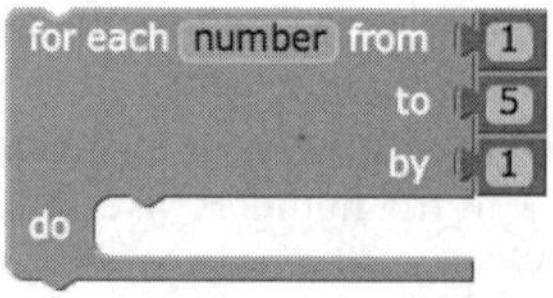

Figure 6.22   The **for each number** loop, as it comes out of the palette.

We use the **number** local variable to step through the length of our lists, repeating an action for each set of items. The action we want repeated is the creation of a row of text, which you can see in Figure 6.23. Don't worry—we explain how it works shortly.

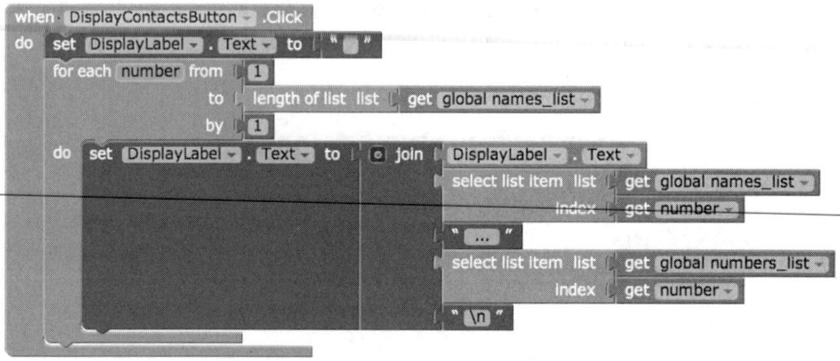

Figure 6.23   Displaying each contact on its own line, using the data from both lists, in a loop.

Let's unpack Figure 6.23. First, all of this happens when the **DisplayContactsButton** is clicked. That's a straightforward button event. Inside an event, the blocks are called in top-down order, so the block at the top of the stack is the first one to run. In this case, that involves clearing the **DisplayLabel.Text** by setting it to be empty text.

When the **DisplayLabel** is cleared, we can start the loop. The loop takes three inputs, which define where it will start and stop counting and how much it will count by. We want to start counting at item 1 and end at the last item of the list, so we have to ask the list how long it currently is, using the **length of list** block. Both lists are the same length (we made sure of that by always adding things to them together), so we can ask either list for length.

Inside the **for each number** loop, the current number is referred to by the orange variable **number**.

So for each item in the list, we want to update the text in the **DisplayLabel**. The first item we'll join together is the existing text in the **DisplayLabel**, the **DisplayLabel.Text**. If we don't include this, each new item will overwrite the previous one, so we'll see only the final entry on the screen, not all of them.

Next, we join the name of the current contact entry. We have the entry number in the local variable number, so to get that entry's name, we just need to pull that number item out of the **names_list**. Easy enough. We do the same for the **numbers_list**, but not before putting in a little bit of text as a spacer (...).

The last part of the text join is a special piece of text, **\n**, which creates a new line. Without this, all the entries will be jammed together on one line. The **\n** is literally a line break, similar to using Return or Enter on the keyboard.

So for each contact entry, this list will display one line for the entry. Pretty cool.

A really convenient feature of storing data like this is how easy it is to get to a certain column. You have all the names in one list, so if you want to use a ListPicker to pick a name, you only have to pass in the existing **names_list** (see Figure 6.24). This way, the ListPicker shows only the names from the contacts.

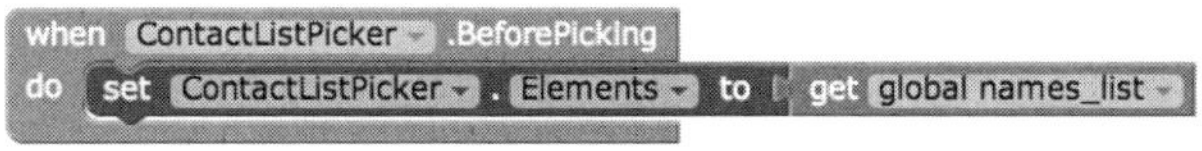

Figure 6.24   Setting up the ListPicker with the current list of names.

After the user picks a name, we want to display the correct number for that person. We'll use another feature of the ListPicker, the **SelectionIndex** property. Whenever a selection is made, the ListPicker saves the item that was picked in a property called **selection** (which we used earlier in this chapter) *and* saves the number of the item in the **SelectionIndex** property.

We need to find the correct number based on which name was picked. The numbers are in a separate list than the names, but we know that the index numbers match up, so the **SelectionIndex** will tell us which item out of the **numbers_list** we want. We will select that item and display it for our user (see Figure 6.25).

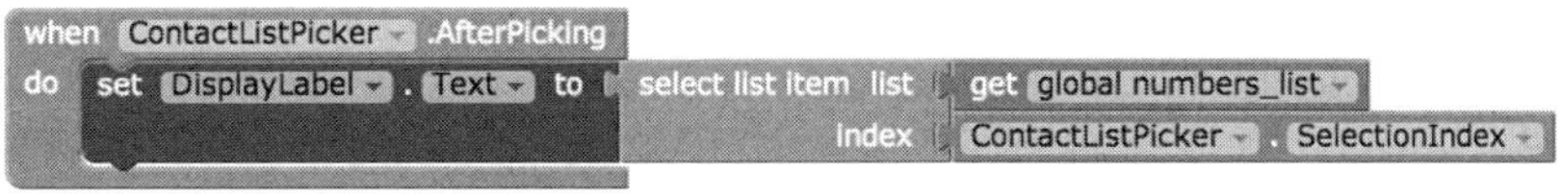

Figure 6.25   Displaying the number that corresponds to the name that was picked in the ListPicker.

That's it! With that small amount of code, we have a basic contact storage and retrieval system using two lists.

Abstraction with Lists and Procedures

Let's use the same example from the earlier section: a phone book contact entry. This time, we're going to implement it with lists as a data structure and then make a list of our structure objects. Remember, each entry will contain a person's name and phone number. So our list that represents a single entry will have two items: a name and a number.

In this example, we're going to design the data structure and build some small procedures to help us manage it so that our code blocks will be easier to read and understand.

Procedures are another way to abstract ideas into simpler containers, with the details hidden. In this case, we'll make one procedure that creates an address book entry and make two procedures to get data out of an address book entry. For more on procedures, refer to Chapter 5, "Procedures."

To make our **Create Entry** procedure, we first need a procedure definition block, from the purple Procedures palette. Use the mutator (the blue gear) to add two inputs, as in Figure 6.26.

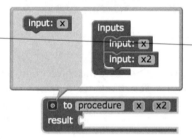

Figure 6.26   The mutator creates a new procedure with two different inputs.

Be sure that you use the procedure with **result**, the one with the result socket. Of course, we need to rename the procedure and the inputs. This procedure is going to construct an address book entry, so we should call it **make_entry**. The inputs are what will be in the entry, so we need to name them to describe what we want: the name and number. You can rename the inputs in the mutator by clicking their names. When you're done, it should look like Figure 6.27.

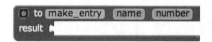

Figure 6.27   The renamed **make_entry** procedure, with inputs for name and number.

To make this procedure work, all we're going to do is create a new list and plug it into the result socket. Hover over the input names, and a pop-up appears, allowing you to grab a getter block for it. Figure 6.28 shows the finished procedure definition block, along with the block that was created to call, or use, the procedure. The procedure now appears in the Procedures flyout palette.

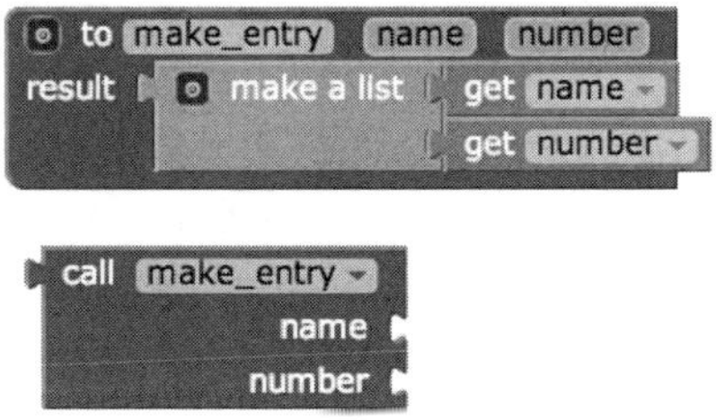

Figure 6.28   The finished **make_entry** procedure definition and the call block that will use it.

To use **make_entry**, we drag out the call block and give it the name and number we want to be stuck together into an entry object. That block then creates a new entry and delivers it out of its left-facing result socket.

Imagine a contacts app that remembers people and their associated numbers. That app would probably have an Add Contact button or screen. Whenever that feature was used, behind the scenes, the **make_entry** procedure would be called to generate a new entry object based on the information the user gave to the app. The code might look something like Figure 6.29.

Figure 6.29   Using **make_entry** to create a new entry object from text the user provided.

But that code isn't done! We need to put that new entry somewhere, and we'll do this in the next section. In the meantime, we need to make the opposite-direction procedures to get the data back out of our entry, as in Figure 6.30. These procedures use the same technique from Figure 6.19; we know that the name will always be item 1 and the number will always be item 2. How do we know this? Because that's what the matching **make_entry** procedure will always do. As long as they agree, we don't have to worry about which entry is which.

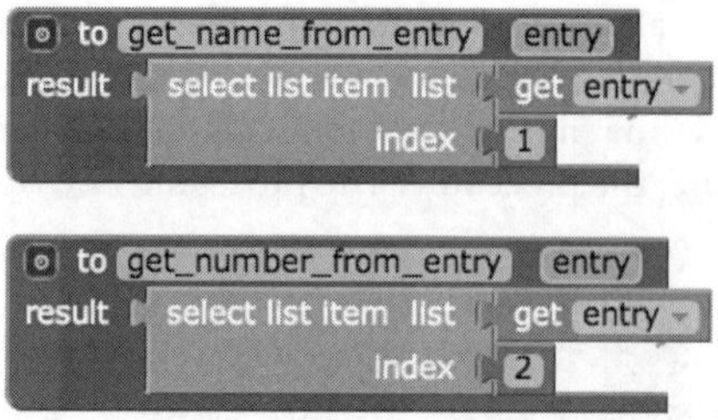

Figure 6.30   The procedures to get information out of a contact entry structure.

Lists that Expand on Demand

In most of this book, we've kept all our data either in properties of components or in global variables. These work great, but they have a limitation: They can't expand. Sometimes we don't know how much information we will need to store, and that's another great use for lists.

The one-dimensional list we discussed earlier in this chapter is perfect for when we need our information to grow. With just one list, we can store any number of items in it.

Consider the contacts app we started imagining in the last section. The user might have 5 friends, or 50, or 500; our app should be able to handle all of them with no problem.

Clearly, we can't make a global variable for each contact. We can't guess how many friends the person will have, and even if we could, we don't want to have to make 500 global variables ourselves. A much easier way to do it is to make a single list and have the list expand every time the user adds a new contact.

So let's make a single list and put in a global variable. Let's give it a good name that describes that it's a list of contacts (see Figure 6.31).

Figure 6.31   Initializing the list that will expand to fit all our data.

We'll use the same text boxes we imagined back in Figure 6.29 as our input. We'll also make a button that we'll use as the action to add the new entry to the list. Put together, it looks like Figure 6.32.

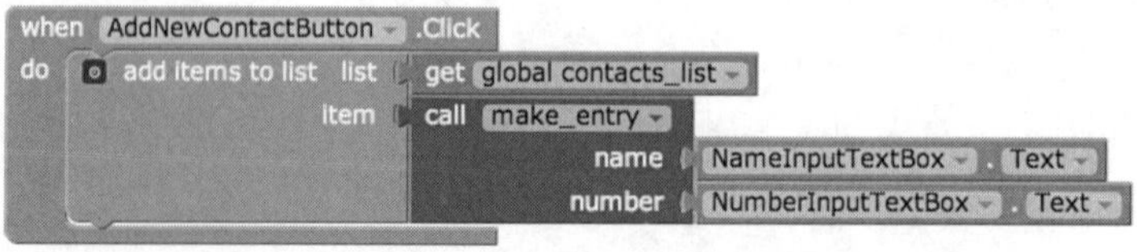

Figure 6.32   When the button is clicked, create a new contact entry and add it to the list.

The app will look exactly the same as an earlier version (refer to Figure 6.21). The user can enter contacts one at a time; then when the user presses the Display Contacts button, the app will show all the contacts, each on a separate line inside a label. Let's see how the new display code works.

The key to remember is that we can't know in advance how many items will be in the contacts list. Whatever the current length of the list is, that's how many items we need to display. We get to use a great control structure, the **for each** loop.

The **for each** loop, from the built-in control palette (see Figure 6.33), is a tool to repeat an action. It repeats the action once for each item in the list that you give it.

Figure 6.33   The **for each** loop, as it comes out of the palette.

The idea here is, for each contact entry in the contacts list, you create a line of text in the label. Creating the line of text is easy. You join a few pieces of text with the **join** block. Then you set the text of the label to be your newly constructed text. Figure 6.34 shows the finished code.

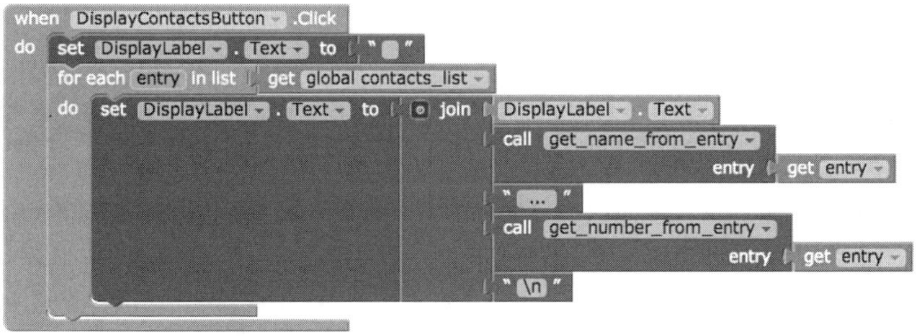

Figure 6.34   The completed action for displaying each entry as its own line in the **DisplayLabel**.

Let's unpack Figure 6.34. First, all of this happens when the **DisplayContactsButton** is clicked. That's a straightforward button event. Inside an event, the blocks are called in a top-down order, so the block at the top of the stack is the first one to run, which in this case is **DisplayLabel.Text**, by setting it to be empty text.

After the **DisplayLabel** is cleared, we can start the loop. The loop takes one input: a list. That list is the **contacts_list**, and it will run its body code (in the "do" section) once for each item in that list. Now let's move on to what happens for each item.

Inside the **for each** loop, the current item is referred to by the orange variable **item**, which you can rename. In this case, it was renamed to **entry** because that's what each item is, a contact entry object that was created with our **make_entry** procedure (remember that?).

So for each item in the contacts list, we want to update the text in the **DisplayLabel**. The first item we'll join is the existing text in the **DisplayLabel**, the **DisplayLabel.Text**. If we don't include this, each new item will overwrite the previous one, so we'll see only the final entry on the screen, not all of them.

Next, we want to join the name of the current contact entry. We have the entry in the local variably **entry**, so we just need to hand that to the procedure **get_name_from_entry**, and we have the name. Easy enough. We do the same thing for **get_number_from_entry**, but not before adding a little text as a spacer (...).

The last item in the text join is a special piece of text, **\n**, which creates a new line. Without this, all the entries will be jammed together on one line. The **\n** is literally a line break, similar to pressing Return or Enter on the keyboard.

Common Problems

A few common issues arise when working with lists. In this section, we talk about the two biggest mistakes.

Running Off the End of the List

Lists can expand as you add more items to them, but at any time, they are finite. It is possible to ask for an item number that is beyond the end of the list (usually using the **select list item** block), and this generates an error that is visible to the user on the phone, such as the one in Figure 6.35. If you are connected in Live Mode, you will also see the error in App Inventor in the browser (see Figure 6.36).

If you read the whole error description, it tells you a lot about what went wrong. First, it's telling you which block failed (in this case, the **select list item** block). It attempted to get list item 5, but the list had only four items. It even shows you what *is* in that list so you can figure out which list it's talking about.

Errors such as this disappear off the phone after a moment but stay visible in the browser until you dismiss them.

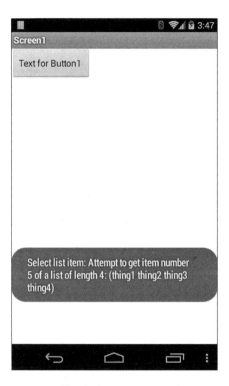

Figure 6.35   A list error, as seen on the device.

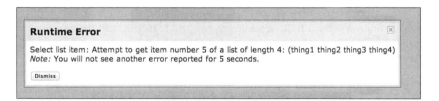

Figure 6.36   A list error, as seen in App Inventor in the browser (when in Live Mode).

So what should you do? Any time you are getting an item from a list by number, you need to make sure that you can't ask for a number larger than the list. Remember, you have tools to help you, including the **length of list** block. If the number you are about to ask for is greater than the length of the list, something is wrong; you need to figure out what you want to do about it. Figure 6.37 shows a template of one way to check that you won't go out of bounds.

The **if** is asking whether the **item_num** is greater than the length of the list. If the answer is yes, you need to correct the issue in the **then** section. If the answer is no, then you're asking for a valid item, and you can go ahead and select it in the **else** section.

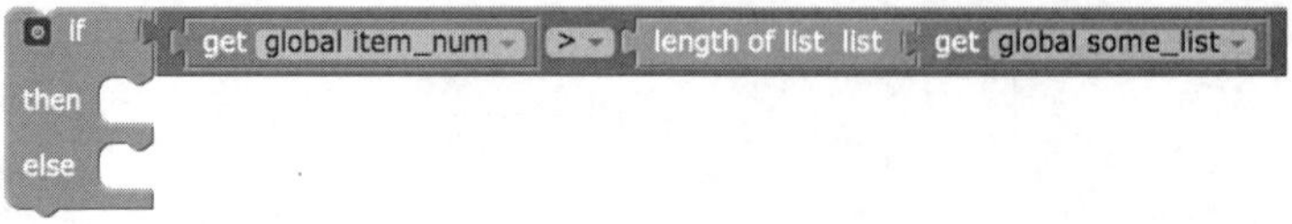

Figure 6.37   One way to check to make sure you don't go beyond the end of the list.

You have many ways to make sure you don't go beyond the end of the list—this is just one. The previous example that used the **for each** loop (the one that iterates over items and doesn't count numbers) is also guaranteed never to go over because it makes sure it does the action only once for each item.

Defining a Variable That Depends on Runtime Elements

Variables are great. Sometimes you can initialize them and include the data as part of the initialization, such as with a hard-coded piece of text (see Figure 6.38). This kind of data is already known before the app starts because it's right there in the code blocks.

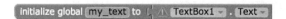

Figure 6.38   A perfectly fine global variable initialization that depends on known information.

However, sometimes you want to fill a variable from data that isn't definitely known or that is somewhere else, such as in a TextBox. If you try to initialize a variable to include data from a component, it doesn't work (see Figure 6.39).

Figure 6.39   An illegal global variable initialization trying to access a component. Components aren't available until later in the startup process.

In Figure 6.39, App Inventor created an error flag, shown as the red triangle. If you click this, it returns "This block cannot be in a definition." This is absolutely true, and here's why.

When your app first starts up, the global variable initializations are done first. This happens before any events take place, before any components are shown on the screen, and before the user even sees the app. At this time, the other components aren't ready yet.

After the global variables are initialized, all the other components come into existence, and the app is running. The very first event that runs is **Screen.Initialize**. After that event completes, all the other events (button presses, canvas flings, and so on) are able to run. The **Screen1.Initialize** event handler is in the Screen1 flyout palette in the Blocks Editor.

This whole startup process is quick, so to the user, it is just a blink of the eye. But you can't use something that's not ready yet. If you try to use a component in a global initialization, it doesn't work. The component won't be ready in time for the global initializations to take place.

If you want a variable to hold data from a component, or do something like Figure 6.39, here's how: Initialize the variable to something (blank or zero—anything that's a known value); then, during the screen's **Initialize** event, set the variable to whatever you want. Figure 6.40 shows this technique.

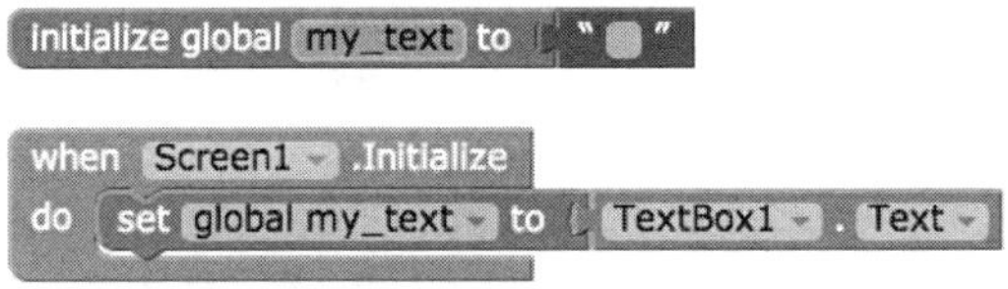

Figure 6.40   The right way to initialize a global using a component (the correct way to do what was shown in Figure 6.39).

This technique initializes the variable with *something*, with the intention to overwrite it with what you actually want later in the startup process, after the components become available. It will look exactly the same to the rest of your code—and your user.

Exercise: Android Quiz

The next project is a quiz app. The user will see a question and type in an answer (see Figure 6.41). We will store the questions and answers in corresponding lists. We'll also need a variable to keep track of what question we are on.

Figure 6.41   The Android Quiz app will make use of lists.

The name of the app is Android Quiz—it will be a five-question quiz to test knowledge about the green robot. Additionally, the app will provide other opportunities for customization and gaining further experience with lists.

1. To begin, create a new project and name it AndroidQuiz. Download the **KitKatLogo** from the companion site and upload it as Media into the App Inventor project.

2. Next, grab the following components and put them together as in Figure 6.42:

   - Label for the title

   - Image for the big Kit Kat logo

   - Label, named **QuestionLabel**, to contain the question

   - Horizontal arrangement (to contain the Answer text box and Answer button, next to each other)

   - Text box for Answer (in the horizontal arrangement)

   - Button to submit answer, named **AnswerButton** (in the horizontal arrangement)

- Label, named **CorrectIncorrectLabel**, to report whether the answer was correct

- Button, named **Next**, to advance to the next question

It's okay if the colors are different. We changed the color of the Answer button in the properties panel to make it stand out. You can do whatever you think works for your app.

Figure 6.42   The AndroidQuiz app in the Designer.

3. Now that the design is complete, it is time to program the blocks. (Keep in mind that when you are designing your own apps, it doesn't work like this. You don't "design, then program." You go back and forth, making changes little by little. Remember that—little by little.)

4. The first task is to create two lists: one for questions and one for answers. To accomplish this, you need to initialize two global variables. Name them **QuestionList** and **AnswerList**.

5. Next, we must fill the lists with our data—the questions and answers. Using the two lists you just created, fill in the questions and answers with text blocks, as in Figure 6.43. (Remember, you can increase the number of sockets using the blue gear mutator.)

Tip

You can also speed up the process by adding blocks through typing. If you type onto the Blocks Editor background, App Inventor will suggest possible blocks that match what you type. Start typing the first few letters of the command and then select it from the list. This even works when adding text: just type a quotation mark and press Enter (see Figure 6.44).

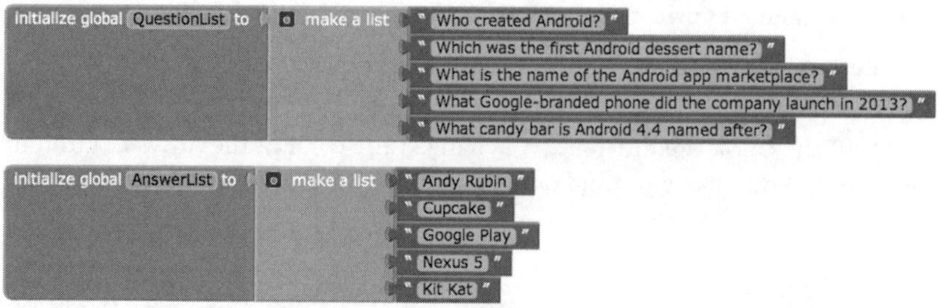

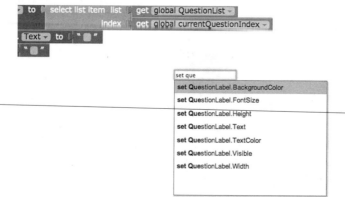

Figure 6.43   The **QuestionList** and **AnswerList**, holding our question data.

Figure 6.44   Typing on the background lets you quickly find blocks.

6. Simply having the questions and answers in a list isn't enough. We need to build the mechanics to display them and change them. We do that by having one combination of blocks that will choose a question from the list and display it in the QuestionLabel. The way we display the text is to set the **Text** property of the QuestionLabel, and it will immediately appear on the screen (see Figure 6.45).

Figure 6.45   The blocks to display one question from the list in the label. This one always selects the first item from the list.

7. The blocks in Figure 6.45 use the **select list item** block to retrieve an item from the list. It currently has the number 1 set as the index, so it always pulls the item at index 1, or the first item, from the list. This is exactly what we want to do when the app first starts

up because the user then will see the first question when the app opens. Put this block in the **Screen1.Initialize** event to make sure it happens when the app starts, as in Figure 6.46. (See the section "Defining a Variable That Depends on Runtime Elements" for more on the **Initialize** event.)

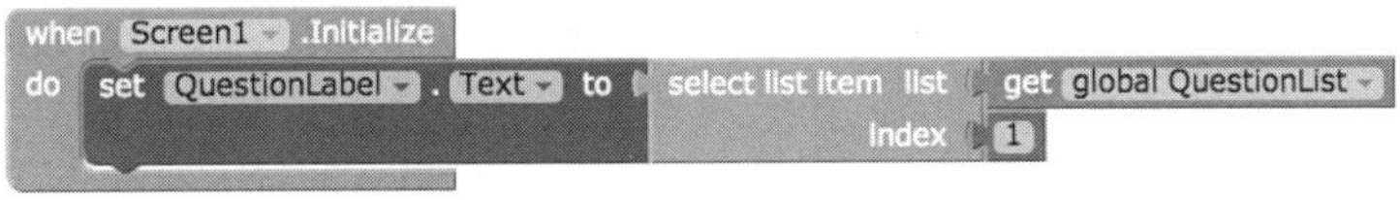

Figure 6.46   Using **Screen1.Initialize** to display the first question when the app starts.

8. We now have the capability to pick a certain question and display it. What we need is the capability to pick the next question and display it, and attach that to the Next button. The problem is, we don't know what "next" is. Are we at question 1? Then we should go to question 2. Are we at question 4? Then we should go to question 5. We need a variable to keep track of what question we're currently on. Then the Next button would only have to increase the number in the variable and refresh the display to match. Let's start by initializing a global variable to use, as in Figure 6.47.

Figure 6.47   Initializing our variable, which will keep track of what question is being displayed.

9. Duplicate the blocks from Figure 6.45 and replace the hard-coded number 1 with the getter for our new variable. (Remember, the getter can be found by hovering over the variable name in the declaration block, or in the Variables built-in menu.) This does the particular combination of blocks: It no longer always displays the first item—it instead displays whichever item index is in the variable. That way, we can change the variable, and the code blocks will display the question to match. See Figure 6.48.

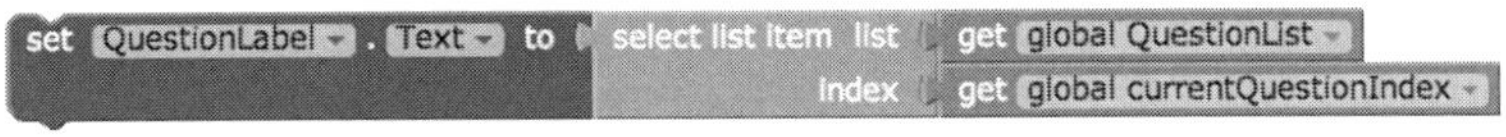

Figure 6.48   Displays the question from the list at whatever index is currently in the variable **currentQuestionIndex**.

10. Now we have the pieces to make the Next button work. Every time the Next button is clicked, we want to first increment the variable by one and then display the question to match, as in Figure 6.49.

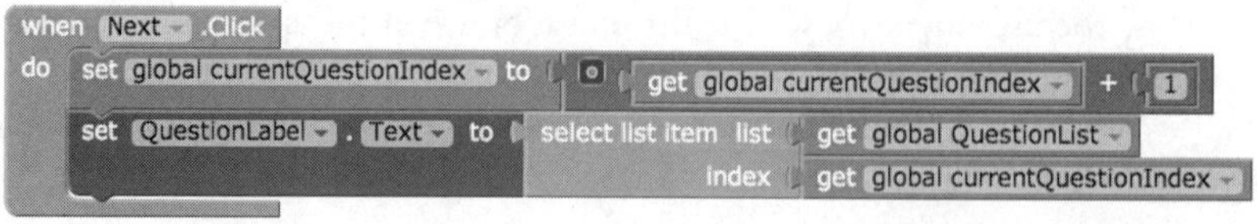

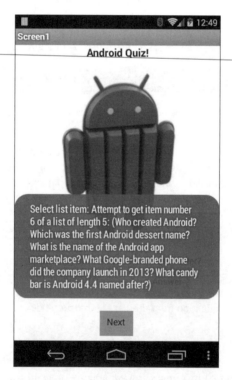

Figure 6.49   The Next button now increments the variable and updates the question.

11. Test the app as we have it so far. Make sure your device is connected, and try the Next button. It will work until you get to the last question; then pressing Next one more time gives you Figure 6.50. You have run off the end of the list, and App Inventor doesn't have the data you've asked for, so you get an error. It says so right in the error text: "Select list item: Attempt to get item number 6 of list length 5…." You have only five items in the list, but you asked for item number 6. Time to add a check—and a fix—for this, as in Figure 6.51.

Figure 6.50   An error occurs on the device because we let our variable go beyond the end of the list.

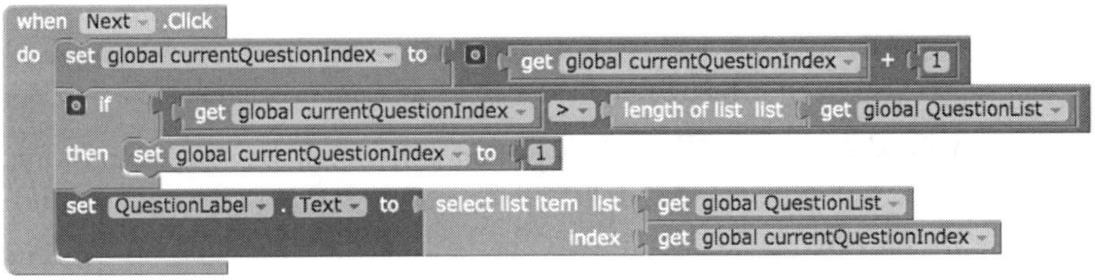

Figure 6.51 An updated **Next.Click** event, adding a check to make sure we don't go beyond the question list and, if we do, to cycle back to the first question.

> **Tip**
>
> You might notice that the only way to reset the variable to 1 is to reset the connection with the app and reconnect. This takes time and is annoying to do. You do have a better way. Grab a setter for the **currentQuestionIndex** variable and give it the number 1 as an input. Don't put this in any event handler—you don't want to include it in the app. When you want to test the Next button, just right-click the floating setter and select Do It from the menu. This instantly sets the variable's value to 1, and the Next button will continue to work. Do It often comes in handy for debugging and testing.

12. Now let's make the AnswerButton check the answer the user typed in. This one is pretty easy. We use the same index variable, **currentQuestionIndex**, to look up the answer to the current question and then compare it against the text in the Answer box. If they're the same, we'll set a display label to read Correct; if not, the label will read Try Again!. You can see this in Figure 6.52.

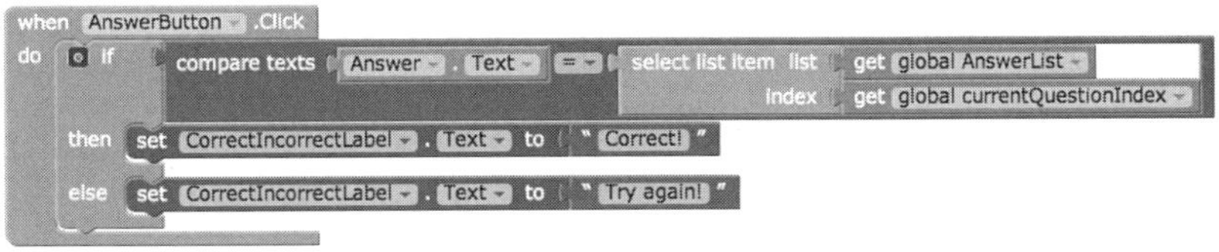

Figure 6.52 When AnswerButton is clicked, compare the text in the Answer box to the correct answer from the list. Display a message of Correct! if they match and Try again! if they don't.

13. Test the app again. Really play with it. Make sure everything works how you want. Try to find the reason for any issues.

14. You will likely encounter one last issue. When you go to the next question, the answer box and the correctness label keep the text from the previous question. This means you have to delete the answer yourself when the question advances. We have an easy fix for this: We need to set the label and text box's text properties to be empty whenever we change questions. The only way to change questions is when Next is clicked, so we'll add it to that event (see Figure 6.53).

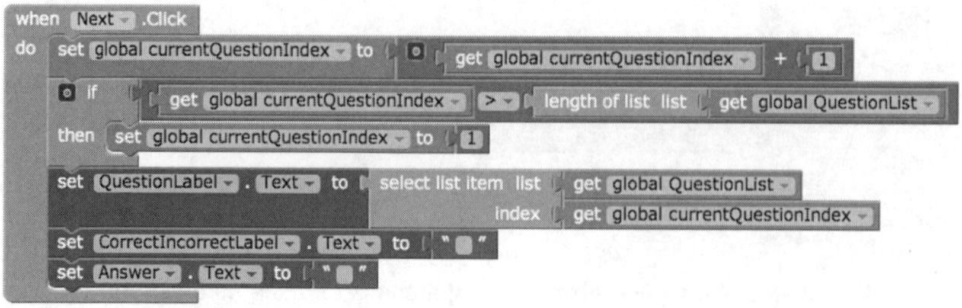

Figure 6.53   The **Next.Click** event updated to clear the **CorrectIncorrectLabel** and the **Answer** text for each question.

Keep in mind that the answers are case sensitive. For example, if the user types in **cupcake** instead of **Cupcake**, the answer will be wrong.

That's it! You now have a small quiz app and (hopefully) a better understanding of lists.

Additional Exercises

1. Try changing some of the questions and answers to the Android Quiz app. Doing so should not change any part of how the app functions—you are simply changing data.

2. Add questions and answers to the quiz. What do you have to change to make them appear?

3. Make the answers non–case sensitive so that **cupcake** and **Cupcake** will both be correct. You can do this without changing the question or answer text.

4. Add an image to go with each question, and have the picture on the screen change when the question changes.

Summary

Lists are a powerful and versatile tool for programming. They can help you keep track of any number of entries, or they can work as small data structures to organize related pieces of data. You can grow or shrink them, select them, print them, and manipulate them in many other ways.

The Android Quiz app makes use of lists and can serve as a practical example for further exploration. If you still find the list-making process somewhat fuzzy, you might want to review the steps in this app. In future apps with larger data sets, you will see that efficient use of lists is important.

This chapter covers many concepts and techniques. You might have to read through it multiple times as your App Inventor skills grow before everything sinks in. Lists are awesome, providing you flexibility and power that you will appreciate more and more as you grow as a programmer.

Games and Animations

Games are one of the most popular genres of mobile apps. MIT App Inventor offers many features that enable a user to create some powerful games, including Pong clones, whack-a-mole games, and a large variety of other game types.

Many of the animation elements that are used in games can also be used for other kinds of apps. This chapter explores these elements in depth, culminating with the step-by-step creation of a golf game. After completing this task, you should have a good foundation for what you can achieve with these components and blocks.

Adding Animations

As the name implies, animations bring your apps to life. Modern smartphone apps are very interactive—they no longer host a stagnant palette of buttons or text. Mastering the animations components and blocks in App Inventor will go a long way toward making your app comparable with the kinds of choices available in the Google Play Store. To understand how to add animation to your apps, you should be familiar with the types of animations available in App Inventor.

We already dabbled with the three components in the Drawing and Animations section while building Flick. We created a ball on a canvas that could be flicked around the screen or moved with the accelerometer (see Figure 7.1).

All the animations are placed on the canvas. The canvas is really an invisible coordinate grid of pixels. Placing or moving the sprites along the canvas can correspond to a value of x or y. The larger the x value, the farther to the right the location is on the screen. The larger the y value, the farther down the location is on the screen.

Changing these values becomes important when it comes time to place sprites and make them interact with others.

Sprites are animated objects. App Inventor uses two sprites: the ImageSprite and the ball.

Figure 7.1   The Drawing and Animation components.

ImageSprite

The ImageSprite component reacts to touches and drags, and it can interact with other image sprites. To use it, you must place it on a canvas.

An ImageSprite is a small image that is on the canvas. You can change what picture the ImageSprite shows, both in the Designer and in the Blocks Editor. A basic example of changing the picture is a 2D game in which the character can go left or right. You might want to switch to a right-facing image for the sprite when it is traveling right and then to left-facing when going left. The ImageSprite can also be set to rotate or not. When set, the picture of the ImageSprite appears to rotate to match the ImageSprite's heading. When unset, regardless of the ImageSprite's heading, the image always appears to have the same rotation as uploaded.

The ImageSprite can also move on the canvas on its own. If you give it a speed and a heading, it will move at that speed in the direction of that heading, until either you stop it or it reaches the end of the canvas. This is useful because you don't have to move it explicitly every frame. Simply tell it to go in this direction at this speed, and it does.

The ImageSprite has some interesting events, too. An ImageSprite can detect being touched, dragged, and flung by the user. It can detect colliding with other sprites on the canvas and can detect hitting an edge of the canvas. It also has some interesting procedures. The purple procedure blocks include tools for instantly moving the ImageSprite to a specific place on the canvas (MoveTo) and instantly rotating to point at a specific coordinate or other sprite (PointInDirection and PointTowards). Be sure to check out all the blocks that are available as you play with what an ImageSprite can do.

Now let's talk about the speed of an ImageSprite. Two properties are involved: **Speed** and **Interval**. To have it move 10 pixels to the left every 1,000 milliseconds (1 second), you would set the **Speed** property to 10 pixels and the Interval property to 1,000 milliseconds. You likely want your animation to be smoother than moving every 1 second. Remember, this is animation, so the interval is how quickly the sprite is updated. The lower the interval, the more often the sprite will move. The speed refers to how many pixels it will move per interval. For the smoothest animation, you want to set a low interval. If you want big jumps, you want to set a high interval. The total speed you will see on the canvas depends on both factors. See Table 7.1 for more detail. Note that, for all those possibilities, the total motion is the same. The difference lies in how smoothly that motion will happen.

You can think about the interval as the same sort of thing as frames per second, which describes how quickly updates are made. But instead of measuring frames per second, we measure seconds per frame—or, more accurately, milliseconds per frame. Each sprite can have separate settings for this, enabling you to create different behaviors to suit your needs.

Table 7.1 **Various Speed and Interval settings, and the resulting smoothness and total motion. You can change the left two columns, and the right two are the results.**

Inputs		Results	
Speed (pixels moved per update)	Interval (milliseconds between updates)	Number of updates in 1 second (Smoothness)	Total motion over 1 second
10	1,000 (1 second)	1	10 pixels
5	500 (half-second)	2	10 pixels
1	100 (1/10th second)	10	10 pixels

Let's talk about the heading property. A heading value of 0 will point the ImageSprite to the right of the screen. The value is a measure of degrees, rotating counterclockwise. That means a value of 90 will point the ImageSprite straight to the top of the screen, 180 will point it to the left, and 270 will point it toward the screen bottom (see Figure 7.2). You can give any number for a heading, so you can point a sprite any of 360 different directions. If a number valued 360 or higher is given as the heading, App Inventor simply wraps it around the circle. A value of 360 also points straight right, 450 is the same as 90, and so on. Negative numbers are also valid and work the same way, but in the opposite direction.

Ball

The ball is the other sprite component. It works just like the ImageSprite *except* that it doesn't contain a picture. A ball will always be a circle of a single color. You can adjust the paint color and the radius of the ball. Otherwise, a ball is exactly the same as an ImageSprite. You can even specify whether a ball rotates, and its motion will behave accordingly, although you won't see a visual difference (a ball looks the same, regardless of its rotation).

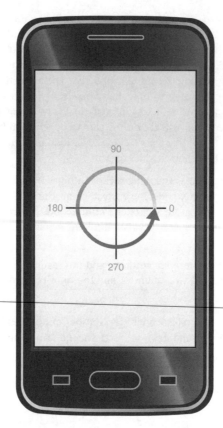

Figure 7.2   Sprite headings on a canvas. Zero points straight right, and as the value increases, the sprite rotates counterclockwise.

Canvas

To use the aforementioned sprites, you need a canvas. As you saw in Flick, this is where you place a sprite or ball.

Basic possible changes include color, width, height, and background image. Additionally, you can specify any location on a canvas as a pair of (x, y) values, where x is the number of pixels away from the left edge of the canvas and y is the number away from the top edge (see Figure 7.3). The maximum values of x and y depend on the size of the canvas, which can vary app to app and from phone to phone. You can always find the maximum values by reading the width and height of the canvas, which you do by getting the **Canvas.Width** and **Canvas.Height** properties, as in Figure 7.4.

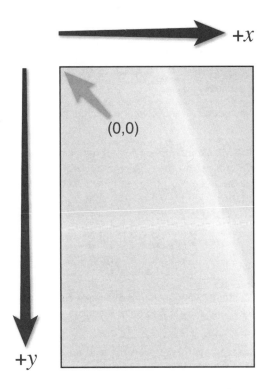

Figure 7.3   The canvas coordinate system. Numbers get larger as they move away from the top-left corner.

Figure 7.4   Getting the canvas width to determine the maximum *x* value for a sprite's location.

Animation Examples

Before we dive into a full-blown app, let's explore a few examples of how these animation components can be used. *This example does not use the built-in speed and heading of the sprite.* You can make a sprite move in many ways, including setting a speed and using a clock.

In Figure 7.5, we have programmed a sprite to move its way vertically across the screen.

For this example, we have placed a ball on a canvas. We also need the Clock, which is an invisible component from the User Interface section of the palette. After putting all these on the Designer, move to the Blocks Editor.

Figure 7.5   The ball will automatically move vertically on the screen.

Fire up the emulator or the AI2 Companion. You will notice the ball moving on its own vertically down the screen. When it gets to the edge, you might want to reset it manually so you can keep experimenting. When you want to reset, put the coordinates you want to reset to in the blocks in Figure 7.6, right-click on it, and select Do It.

Figure 7.6   The ball will instantly jump back to the top-right corner of the screen. Have this block handy so you can right-click it and use Do It to reset the sprite while testing.

Try changing the values to see how this impacts the ball movement. Additionally, explore making the ball move diagonally. Do this by giving the x and y variable the same value.

Smoother Animation

You might have noticed that the animation in the last sequence isn't exactly the smoothest. Fortunately, you have a remedy for this. In the Properties box from the Designer, click Clock and look at the TimerInterval box (see Figure 7.7).

Properties
Clock1
TimerAlwaysFires ☑
TimerEnabled ☑
TimerInterval 1000

Figure 7.7   The **TimerInterval** property of the Clock component.

Reducing the value causes the sprite to refresh more regularly and provides smoother scrolling across the screen instead of a choppy effect. Changing the **TimerInterval** property of the Clock in this section works exactly the same as changing the ImageSprite's interval, as we discussed in the section "ImageSprite." The lower the interval, the more often the update and the smoother the behavior.

Edges and Collisions

Another way to affect movement with sprites is through the blocks that control edges and collisions.

In the Flick app, we used the **whenEdgeReached** block to tell the ball to bounce off the edges.

A similar effect is used for collisions. Given that many games have collisions, this kind of permission comes in handy. Event handlers in the ImageSprite and the ball report when sprites collide with each other on the canvas and let you handle that collision however you want. If you specify nothing, they will pass through each other. The "collision" still happens, but no behavior change occurs. You must specify any behavior change you want, and it can be whatever you like.

Exercise: Fore

A golf course is a challenge because of its obstacles, so it makes a good model for an app when we want to practice working with edges, collisions, palettes, and sprites.

Create a new project and name it Fore. We are then going to become golf course architects and design the first hole.

1. We need the following elements: a canvas, two balls, and a clock.

2. The canvas should fill the screen: Set the width to Fill Parent and the height to 400 pixels. Then make the background green.

3. Make the ball white and give it a radius of 8 (or whatever you find makes the best size for flicking across the screen—see Figure 7.8).

4. We need to adjust the Z value for the ball in the Properties box—make it 2.0. We need this because this ball must appear on top of the other ball, which we will use as the hole.

5. Next, we want to program the GolfBallFlung event handler. This block will use several different arguments to make the ball perform the way we want when the user flings it.

6. We can vary the speed in the Math block. Start with 5, but be willing to tweak it later to see how it impacts the speed of the ball (see Figure 7.9).

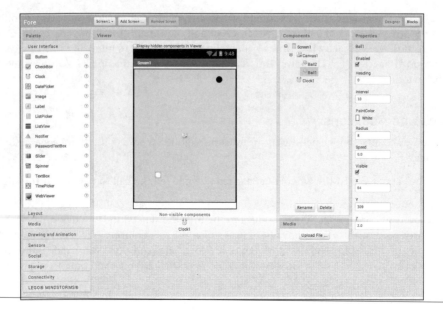

Figure 7.8   The canvas with a ball sprite for the hole and a ball sprite for the golf ball.

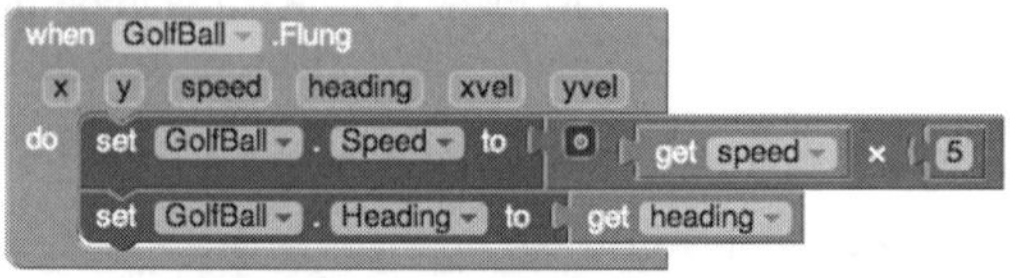

```
when  GolfBall ▾ .Flung
      x   y   speed   heading   xvel   yvel
do    set  GolfBall ▾ . Speed ▾ to   0    get  speed ▾   ×   5
      set  GolfBall ▾ . Heading ▾ to   get  heading ▾
```

Figure 7.9   Programming the ball behavior to react properly to being flung.

7. Now we need to program the behavior of the clock, which will slow the ball after it rolls
   for a while. In the Clock1 flyout menu, choose whenClock1Timer. Now grab an **if then**
   block and use the mutator to add an **else** case. Remember to click the blue button and
   then drag the phrase **else** into the empty block (see Figure 7.10).

Figure 7.10   Adding an **else** case to the **if** block in the mutator pop-up.

8. If you try out the app, you will see that flicking the ball sends it across the screen: It zips across the canvas for a while and then slows down, or it comes to a sudden stop when it hits the edge. Figure 7.11 shows where the blocks should be at this point.

Figure 7.11   The completed set of blocks with the Clock1 timer and ball fling.

9. To fix the issue of the ball stopping on the wall, program what is shown in Figure 7.12. This is the first step in ensuring that the ball will bounce off the edges instead of sticking to them.

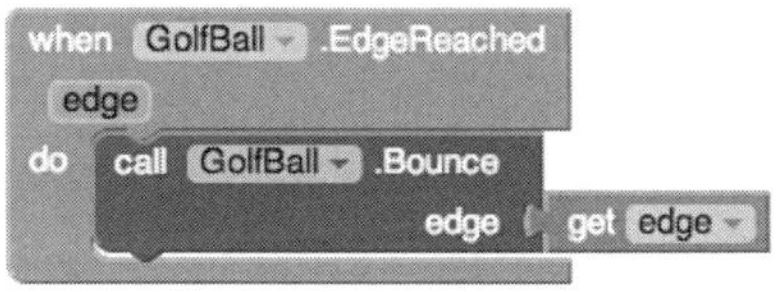

Figure 7.12   Programming the ball to bounce off the edges.

10. Now we can create a procedure that relocates the hole after the ball has been knocked in. Grab the **to** procedure and name it **newhole**. We then can add some of the math blocks and variables for the purpose of adjusting its performance (see Figure 7.13).

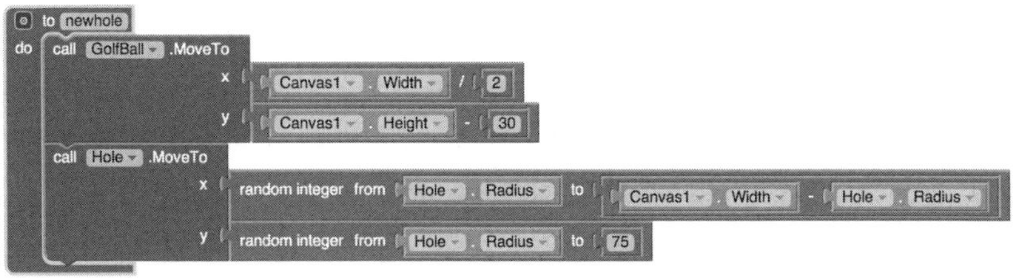

Figure 7.13   Writing a new procedure to reset the game to a new hole. This procedure will be called when the ball goes in the hole.

11. Now we need to finish this step, which sends the ball back to the bottom of the screen. Program what you see in Figure 7.13, paying specific attention to the placement of the math blocks.

12. Figure 7.14 involves several different blocks, including an **if then**, math, and procedures. This tells the app to place the ball back at the beginning when you have successfully shot the ball into the hole.

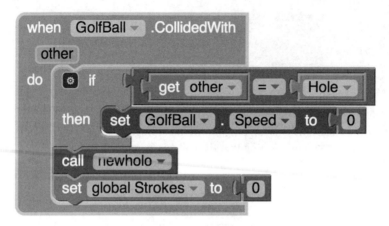

Figure 7.14   When the GolfBall collides, check whether it is colliding with the Hole. If it is the Hole, then run the **newhole** procedure to reset the game.

13. Try the app to be sure it is doing what we have programmed it to do: When the golf ball hits the hole, it should be sent back to the bottom of the screen and the hole should be sent to another location. If that is not the case, double-check the code.

Programming the game to keep score is the next step. Grab the following blocks to begin this part of the app-building process. Many different steps are involved in adding this functionality.

1. Place a Horizontal Arrangement table at the top of the screen.

2. Grab two labels and call them Score and Strokes.

3. Go back to the Blocks Editor and create two new variables; call them **Score** and **Strokes**.

4. Next, go back to the blocks with GolfBallFlung on the top.

5. Add the blocks shown in Figure 7.15. This programs the game to keep track of the score and reset the score for the hole during each round.

6. Test the app using the emulator or AI Companion app. You should be able to swipe the ball and watch it "roll" across the screen. The counters at the top of the page will then increase with each fling.

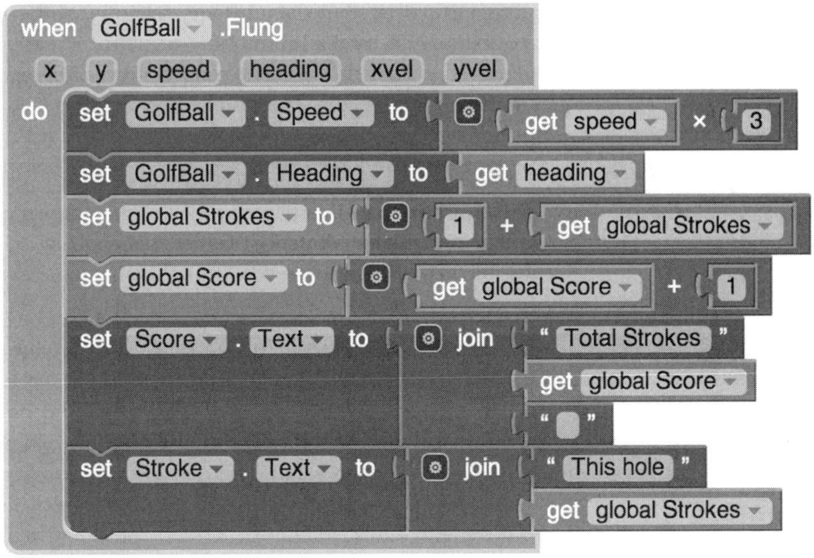

Figure 7.15   Adding scorekeeping to the **Flung** event.

Additional Exercises

This game offers plenty of room for customization. You can change the speed of the ball, change the location of the hole, or add obstacles.

1. Try changing the number of obstacles, adding different ones or moving an existing obstacle to a different location.

2. Add another ball or hole to see how that impacts the game. Explore other ways to change the course, making it more difficult or different from just a standard layout.

3. Add a second screen and complete a new hole from scratch. Later, we explore methods for making good multiscreen apps.

Summary

App Inventor has a number of animation tools that you can use to create some enjoyable games. Our example will hopefully inspire you to try some different kinds of games or other uses of animation to make some interactive apps.

With a good grasp of the use of sprites, timers, collisions, and the other elements covered in this chapter, you are ready to tackle some more in-depth design and engineering strategies.

8

Multiple Screens and Debugging Techniques

To this point, the applications we have built have shared one commonality: They have all had one screen. However, more sophisticated apps—and the ones you likely use every day on your smartphone—make use of many different screens.

By learning a few procedures, you will be able to add multiple screens to your app as well. This chapter discusses the steps for doing so and explores the strengths and limitations of adding multiple screens to an application. The exercises also give you some hands-on experience.

The chapter winds up with a foray into debugging techniques for App Inventor.

Why More Than One Screen?

Apps rarely have all their content on one screen. For example, with news apps, you often must touch a headline or link to be taken to a second page.

Figure 8.1 shows an image from the Android Developer page that provides a sketch of the many factors to consider when developing apps. Users often enjoy interacting with vibrant, colorful icons. In addition, you should consider where the user will need to touch and ways to minimize the taps needed when navigating through an app.

The future of Android's look is in what Google calls Material Design. Think of it as a digital version of a scrapbook, with contrasting colors and clean lines.

Although MIT App Inventor does much of the work for you in terms of design, being aware of where Google and the wider mobile industry are headed with design trends is wise. MIT App Inventor is a good launching pad for learning how to design mobile apps that are both visually appealing and functional.

This chapter focuses on using multiple screens. That requires thinking about design on a higher level: The user will be switching from one interface to another, so the navigation must not be too jarring or inconsistent.

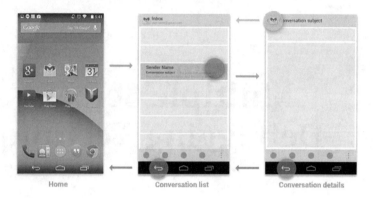

Figure 8.1   Visually compelling apps make for a better user experience.

Building Apps with Multiple Screens

The apps we have built to this point have all used a single screen. Yet most apps that you use likely have multiple screens. This facilitates separating different groups of features, without needing to have all the content crammed onto one page.

However, it is worth spending some time to master this. If not programmed properly, multiple screens can become a source of irritation for users. Programming multiple screens also can be tricky, and finding errors while using multiple screens can be cumbersome. At a few points, you, the programmer, can't undo changes, so mistakes will require you to redo a significant amount of work. Carefully consider the information in this chapter before you design an app that uses multiple screens.

Figure 8.2 shows an example of adding a second screen. By default, it is named Screen2. This naming convention will probably work in most cases, but with specific apps, assigning a name is more useful.

Warning

Once you give a second screen a name, you can't change it.

When adding a second screen, you are presented with the default name, Screen2. Either keep it by pressing OK or give it a different name. Once you give it a name, you cannot change it. Luckily, the name of the screen is not visible to your users, so the name doesn't really matter, as long as you know what it means. If you create a screen and name it Preferences but then realize that you spelled it wrong, don't worry! That name is never seen in the final app, and you can always change any text that is visible onscreen. The same holds true if you create a screen and then change its function. Your Preferences screen might evolve into a social media screen, but the name will always be Preferences if that is what you initially named it. That's not a big deal, again, because the user will never know.

Figure 8.2   Adding a second screen.

What Screens Are Good At

Multiple screens enable you to create separate pages for groups of related features in your app. Consider how a news app must take the user from the main screen with headlines to a page with the specific article. Perhaps a page also exists for setting user preferences. All these can be realized with screens.

As an example, we previously built an application called Android Quiz. Perhaps you want to differentiate the focus of the app, building one page dedicated to a quiz on Android and another page focused on trivia about devices.

Screens help separate functionality. Each screen should house a set of features and functions that are used together and are largely disconnected from the features of other screens.

Screens share media components, such as sounds and pictures. As an example, an image that you uploaded and use in Screen1 can also be used in Screen2 (or any other screen).

Issues with Multiple Screens

Multiple screens make your app more complicated and introduce more possibilities for bugs and errors.

In live development mode, screens can take a long time to switch. This includes using the AI Companion, USB connection, and emulator. When you switch screens in live development mode, the Designer must load all the components and blocks for the new screen and then push them to the phone. This makes testing difficult and often frustrating. Screens change faster when the app is built into an Android package and installed.

In the final app, screens take a moment to switch. They are not intended to be switched rapidly and shouldn't be used when the user wants a feature from both at the same time.

Properly testing screen transitions requires packaging with each change, which adds extra steps and time. Most screen transitions cannot be tested instantly as most features of App Inventor can.

Depending on your design, sharing information between screens is not always easy. Adding multiple screens works only under the right circumstances, so be sure that having the app configured this way is in the best interest of the user.

Screens do not share components, layouts, or any blocks, including variables. When a new screen is created, it's like a whole new app. Anything you write in one screen has to be rewritten in another screen (but if you're rewriting features, that's a good sign that maybe they should be on the same screen!).

> **Warning**
> Screen1 cannot be renamed.

Your app always initially opens in Screen1. You cannot rename or delete Screen1, and you cannot switch it with another screen.

When first using screens, many App Inventor programmers want to add a welcome screen to an existing app and are surprised to find that the welcome screen needs to be in Screen1 and that then it is too late to change that.

Switching Screens

To open another screen, you use the block under the Control palette called **open another screen**. This block requires one input, which must be the name of the screen you want to open, in a text block. See Figure 8.3 for the programming that opens Screen2 when a button is pressed.

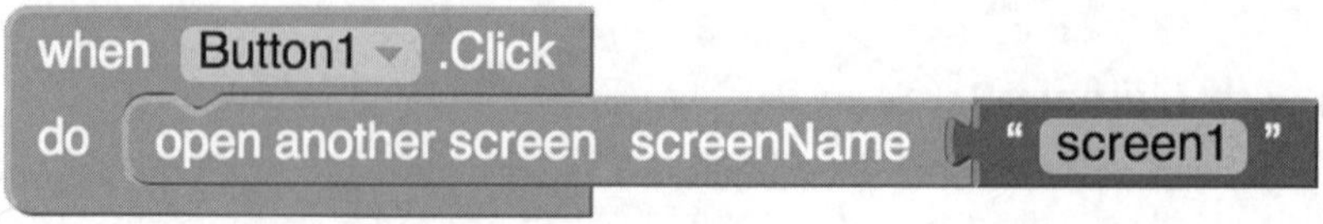

Figure 8.3   Programming an app to switch screens.

Screen behavior is like a small deck of cards on a table. You start with just one card, which is Screen1, the first screen you see. When you open another screen, that screen opens on top of the previous one, like another card being put on the deck (see Figure 8.4).

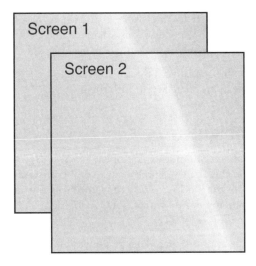

Figure 8.4   Think of multiple screens like a stack of cards.

The best part of this card stack model is that the previous screen is still there—it's just currently hidden and suspended. The right way to go back to the first screen is to use the **close screen** block (see Figure 8.5), which takes the current card off the stack and reveals the previous card underneath. When **close screen** is used from Screen2, Screen2 shuts down and disappears, bringing the user back to Screen1.

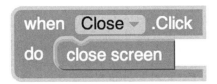

Figure 8.5   Using the **close screen** block.

Sharing Data Between Screens

Screens are like individual apps that you can switch between. They don't share variables or blocks, so getting information from one screen to another takes a little bit of setup.

One of the more convenient ways to get data across screens is to use TinyDB. Anything you store in TinyDB is available in all the screens. TinyDB stores its data on the phone, not in the app itself, so the data in it persists even when the app is closed or screens are switched.

For example, you might have a page where the user can specify settings. Whenever a setting is changed, it gets stored immediately to TinyDB. This way, when the app is closed, those settings are remembered and honored. Now, because it uses TinyDB, those settings can be moved to a new screen, and the app still remembers the settings in every screen.

Of course, to make the settings actually do things, you have to write your app to get that data out of TinyDB and take the appropriate action with them.

Debugging Techniques

Inevitably, something in an app will not work properly or meet expectations. Getting everything in an app to work on the first try is pretty rare. Finding the perfect conversion from your imagination to the reality of the blocks can take time, too. This is where debugging comes in: You must troubleshoot your app to find what's not working right and why, and then you must fix it.

Finding errors while writing apps isn't bad. They're not your fault. You're not a bad programmer for writing buggy code blocks. That's all perfectly normal. What makes you a good programmer is finding and fixing them. This process of debugging is where much of the learning takes place. You'll never understand a feature (of any system) better than after debugging something that uses it. Debugging forces you to have a conversation with the blocks, to listen as well as speak, and your app will be better as a result. Additionally, *you* will be a better programmer because you will have expanded your brain through the problem-solving process.

Leaving Comments

Let's start with the easiest part: commenting. You can right-click any block and choose Add Comment. This creates a blue question mark on the block, which has an attached field of text where you can write whatever you want (see Figure 8.6). This text is for you to leave comments, or notes, on what you're trying to do with the block. No real rules apply here, but keep in mind that the purpose of comments is to help someone understand in the future what you are currently thinking and how your blocks are realizing those thoughts.

Figure 8.6   Adding a comment to a block is a way to leave yourself (or other people) notes to help interpret what your blocks are doing.

You can hide (and unhide) the comment box by clicking the blue question mark. You can also delete the comment entirely by right-clicking the block again and choosing Remove Comment.

Test Small and Test Often

The key to making apps that work is to be constantly testing what you make. Really. Test every little feature as you add it. Nothing is worse than having pages of blocks that you *think* work and then having to pull it all apart when you have an error hiding somewhere in the churning code.

If you write a feature that depends on other pieces to be written before you test it, you might try to get away without testing it. That's a bad move. Figure out a way to test the feature independently of the others. Then you can move forward with confidence.

Do It

App Inventor provides one great tool for testing and debugging: Do It. You can right-click on any block at any time, as long as a device or emulator is connected, and select Do It from the menu. This option runs that block immediately on the device, even if it is not inside an event (see Figure 8.7).

Figure 8.7   Using the Do It feature to immediately run any block.

The Do It feature is simple, and you can use it in many ways, depending on what blocks you have and what you need to test. Here are some examples of how you can use Do It to help with testing and debugging:

- Reset lists (set a list to an empty list)
- Move sprites to start locations
- Start TinyWebDB queries to test the response behavior
- Slowly step through long stacks of blocks, running each block one at a time

- Run any block immediately and see the resulting action on the phone
- For blocks that have result values, show the result on the computer screen after Do It (see Figure 8.8)

Figure 8.8   Using the Do It feature to show the result of a getter block.

Do It has one more great feature. Some blocks have result outputs, a left-facing socket where they deliver a resultant value of some kind when they are called. If you use Do It on these blocks, even if they're not attached to anything, App Inventor will show you the result on the screen. The result is written into a comment, as in Figure 8.8. This is a regular comment with the value inserted. Selecting Do It again updates the value printed.

You can show the result value on any block that has a result socket—it can be just a simple getter block, as in Figure 8.9, or a more complex procedure block. In the latter case, the block will run (it will "be done") only if all its inputs have a value supplied. If input sockets are empty, then it can't run and it can't provide a value.

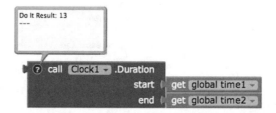

Figure 8.9   Using the Do It feature to show the result of a procedure that returns a result.

Name Well

One of the hardest parts of programming—and computer science—is choosing names. This is no joke—it really is difficult, and it is critically important. No, the computer and phone don't care what you named your button. But for humans, this is a big deal.

Names are more than just a word or two to describe what something does. The process of naming causes you to think about what it *should* do and what it *should not* do. You might have a button named **submit_button**, for example. This name makes it clear to others, and to you, that the button is used in the process of submitting something. It is not for clearing the screen or any other function. It is for submitting.

As another example, a variable might be named **sum**, and that could be a good or bad name. If it is a global variable, someone might ask, what is it the sum of? Maybe it is a local variable inside a procedure, and that procedure takes a list. In such a case, the **sum** might make it perfectly clear that it is the sum of the things in that list.

The procedure itself could have any name. A procedure that sums a list of numbers and returns the result could be named **list_summer**—the name says what it does and implies what the return value represents. If you just call that procedure **summer**, the name then makes it less clear what the procedure does and what the inputs and result should be.

A really good name gives someone reading your blocks an idea of what it *does* without forcing them to study the blocks.

Consider naming to be equivalent to creating a contract: You are deciding what that thing is by giving it a descriptive, succinct name. If you later use that thing for something else, you are breaching the contract. In such a case, it is best to rename the thing to better match the new use of it.

Backing up Your Work

Working in App Inventor can feel much like working in Google Drive, where the program backs up the work automatically. However, this should not lull you into a false sense of security. Backing up your work regularly is still a good practice.

The first option for backing up is to just use the Save button, which is located in the My Projects menu (see Figure 8.10). This simply makes sure the project is saved and does the same thing as autosave. Do this right before you close App Inventor to make sure that autosave didn't miss anything.

Another good practice is to save checkpoints of your project. One example of when this is useful is when you have an app that works, and you want to try something new that could break it. The checkpoint creates a copy of your project in its current state, so if you need to go back in time, you can open the checkpoint project. When you create a checkpoint, you continue working in the original project. Any changes are saved in the original project, but not the checkpoint copy.

Making a checkpoint is almost the same as using Save As, except that with a checkpoint, you continue working in the original file; the new file holds the old state of the project.

To save a checkpoint, choose Checkpoint from the My Projects menu. Then either assign it a name or choose the default option (see Figure 8.11).

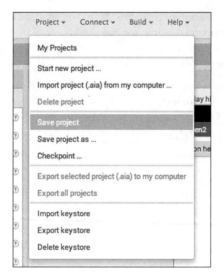

Figure 8.10   The Save Project option.

Figure 8.11   Naming a checkpoint.

The checkpoints are available from the same listing as the rest of the apps. After you create a checkpoint, you can open it at any time. Use checkpoints to save important moments in your development history that you might want to go back to later, such as moments when something works before you try a new feature or change.

Exercise: Pollock Plus One

In the next exercise, we take the existing Pollock app (from Chapter 6, "Working with Lists") and add a second screen. This gives you practice in creating multiple screens and ensuring that you have a path for navigating between the two.

1. Launch Pollock from the My Project page. On the Designer screen, add another button next to the row of buttons devoted to the paint colors.

2. Rename the button to Switch in the components table. Be sure to also change the text for the button in the Properties box. Give it a different color, such as Cyan (see Figure 8.12).

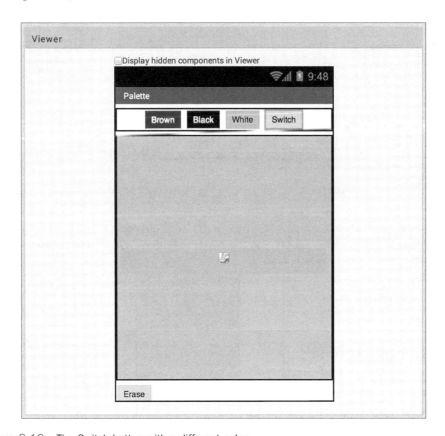

Figure 8.12   The Switch button with a different color.

3. Next, add a second screen. As a reminder, you do this by clicking the Add Screen button. You can keep the name Screen2 or give it another name.

4. In Screen1, go to the Blocks Editor. Program the Switch button to open Screen2 when pressed (see Figure 8.13).

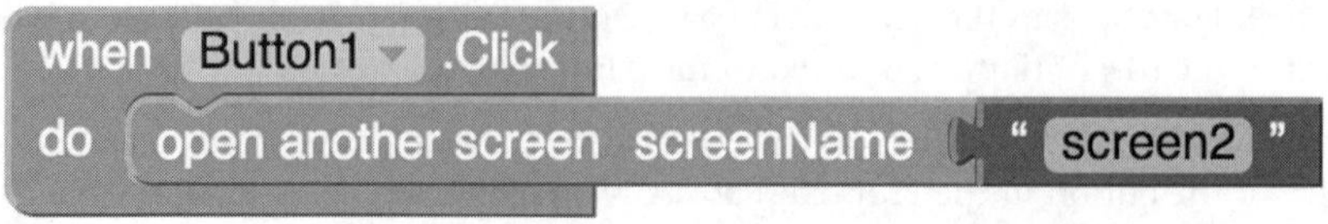

Figure 8.13   Programming the Switch button to open Screen2.

5. From Screen2, add a button that takes you back to Screen1. From the Designer, grab a button and place it in the Viewer. Then program the same behavior as the button from Screen1 (see Figure 8.14).

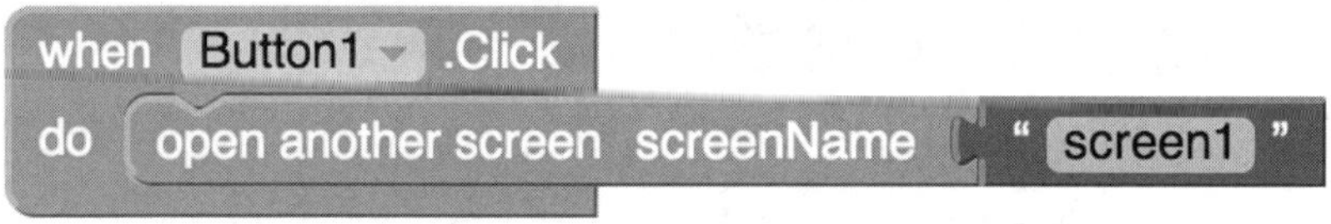

Figure 8.14   Programming the same behavior as the button from Screen1.

6. Now test the behavior with the emulator or AI Companion app. When pressing the button to switch screens, notice that the App Inventor program in your browser switches to match.

7. Review the content from building Pollock in Chapter 6. We used a particular design scheme with an autumn-themed batch of colors.

Additional Exercises

1. Build on one of the previous examples, such as Android Quiz, and add a second screen. Then create a variation of the app's functions from the first screen. Explore how adding multiple screens can enhance any of the apps you have built.

2. The trickiest, and perhaps the most important, function of adding a second screen is connecting it to the first to create a seamless transition. Practice doing so by adding multiple screens to various apps and building interconnectivity between then.

Summary

Using multiple screens is useful in building bigger, more capable apps while keeping the features organized and usable. Screens are good at separating sets of features, but they are bad at sharing data. Using screens takes thought and careful design because you could make a few mistakes that you cannot undo.

For most simple cases, screens are not necessary, and you can fake screenlike functionality by making different sets of components visible and invisible on one screen. This is simpler for the programmer and the Android device, so it is recommended whenever possible.

Debugging is a critical set of skills that develop with programming experience. The Do It feature of App Inventor is a powerful tool for debugging, allowing the programmer to run blocks and query the state of the app instantly in real time, as the app is running. App Inventor also provides a mechanism for leaving comments, enabling you to leave notes to help a future reader of the app understand the thought processes behind the blocks.

Making a good app depends on good debugging. Testing, thinking about good names, and using Do It are the basic skills for debugging in App Inventor.

Using Media

A large percentage of smartphone apps use some type of media. Whether it's audio, video, or images, App Inventor has a way to bring these different media types into your apps.

This chapter explores how to use App Inventor in making media-rich apps, whether through sprinkling in some video or creating an app that focuses primarily on various forms of multimedia.

An entire section of the Designer is devoted to the different media types you can add to an app. We have explored some of them already (primarily the images), but we now look at some different types to include (see Figure 9.1).

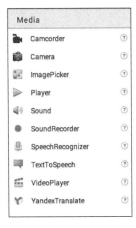

Figure 9.1   The Media palette in the Designer, showing the various media components.

Many of the components for this category are nonvisible (see Figure 9.2). To make them do something, we must program their action to occur based on some other event, such as clicking a button.

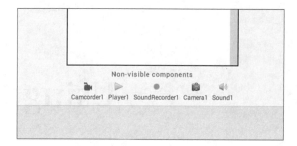

Figure 9.2   Nonvisible components are listed below the Viewer.

Audio

Adding audio requires uploading the specific sound that you want into App Inventor. Recall that, in Chapter 2, "Building with MIT App Inventor," we built the Speak, Android! app. This app used a speech recognition component built into App Inventor.

However, you can add any kind of audio from your computer into an app. Doing so involves one of two audio components: Sound or Player. You can upload sound files directly into the Media section of the Designer, as we have in previous chapters. In addition, you can upload directly in the Sound component's Source property menu, as in Figure 9.3. The Upload File button in the Source menu also uploads the file to the Media section.

Player is best for longer audio files, such as a song. Sound is best for short clips, such as the one we will be using in this demonstration. However, both components can be used to control the vibration of the phone while playing the audio, which is controlled with the Blocks Editor and measured in milliseconds.

To add short audio, drag the Sound component into the Viewer. Notice that this is an invisible component, so no icon appears in the middle of the Viewer (see Figure 9.2).

After adding the element, you must upload the actual sound. As an example, choose the wav1 file from the Learning MIT App Inventor companion site. Next, click the Upload button and send the file from your computer.

Sometimes you might find a file format that doesn't work with the Sound component. When this happens, try it with the Player component. The Player is capable of playing more formats than Sound. If a short sound effect requires a Player, that's fine—it doesn't hurt to use the more powerful tool for your quick sound effects.

Additionally, it is worth checking the Android developer site to determine what media are supported. This could change over time as Google continues its work in building the operating system.

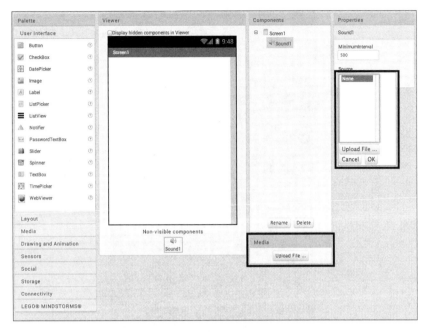

Figure 9.3   You can add a sound file to the app through the Source property menu of a Sound component or by uploading directly into the Media section. Both instances of Upload File end up doing the same thing, but the one in Source automatically attaches it to that component.

Images

You have a couple choices when it comes to working with images: ones that already exist on the device and those you newly create.

The ImagePicker

The ImagePicker enables your user to import some preexisting images into the app. This is great for letting users pick their own profile pictures, backgrounds, or other customizable pictures. Add it just like a button, by dragging it into the Viewer. The ImagePicker looks like a button and has many of the same properties and configurations of a button. When pressed, however, it opens a menu that lets users pick from the Android image library, using their image browsing app of choice (see Figure 9.4).

Figure 9.4   The ImagePicker, when clicked, launches in the image selection app and lets users choose from their existing inventory of images.

After the user selects an image, the file location of that image is stored in the ImagePicker's Selection property, which is accessible only with a green getter block. That file location is suitable for use with any block that takes an image as input, such as setting the Picture that is shown in a Button or Image component.

The following figures show a simple example app that lets the user choose an image with the ImagePicker and then displays that image in an Image component on the screen. In the Designer, it looks like Figure 9.5.

After the user clicks the ImagePicker (which looks like a button), the user gets the picker (refer to Figure 9.4). The user then selects an image, and that image is displayed (see Figure 9.6). Figure 9.7 shows the blocks that make it happen.

Figure 9.5   A simple app that lets the user pick an image and then shows that image.

Figure 9.6   The app showing the image that the user picked.

Figure 9.7   The blocks that take the image the user picked and set it as the picture for the Image component, to display it.

All images and pictures in App Inventor are really filenames, so they can be handled and stored like pieces of text. In this case, **ImagePicker1.Selection** is reporting a piece of text to be stored in **Image1.Picture**, and the Image component knows to go open that file and display it. This is why, when you change images with the blocks, you have to type in the whole name of the image file you uploaded.

This means you can save images just like you can text, such as in a list, in a TinyDB, or in a variable. The filenames refer to the file that holds the actual image.

Of course, you have to worry about a few edge cases. You cannot store an image in TinyWebDB, for example. All that gets stored is the file location on *your device*, so if other users don't have the same file in the same location, they won't be able to see it.

In addition, if the file is included in the Media of the app, as shown at the beginning of this chapter, all the copies of your app will have the same media.

The Web component is capable of transmitting the image data with a **POST** request, but you need to have a server that knows what to do with it, which is far beyond the scope of this book. The Web component can also download images from the Internet, which is a bit easier, using the **GET** request. Turn on the **SaveResponse** property, and the file will be stored on the device; the Web component then will provide you with a text name for that file that you can use just as we have above.

The Camera

Now that you know all about using existing pictures from the device, let's make some new ones. The Camera component activates the camera in the phone and lets the user take a picture using the phone's camera app. After the picture is taken, it returns to your App Inventor app and provides the name of the new picture for you to use.

The Camera component is simple to use, with only one procedure block and one event handler block. The procedure, **TakePicture**, launches the camera application. That's all it does. Any blocks connected beneath it will run immediately. The **TakePicture** block does not wait for the picture to be completed—that could take whole minutes because humans take time to do things. When the user takes and is satisfied with the picture, the **AfterPicture** event triggers. In that event is a parameter image, which holds the name of the new picture file just created. The simplest thing to do is take that image name and put it right on the screen using an Image or Button component (see Figure 9.8).

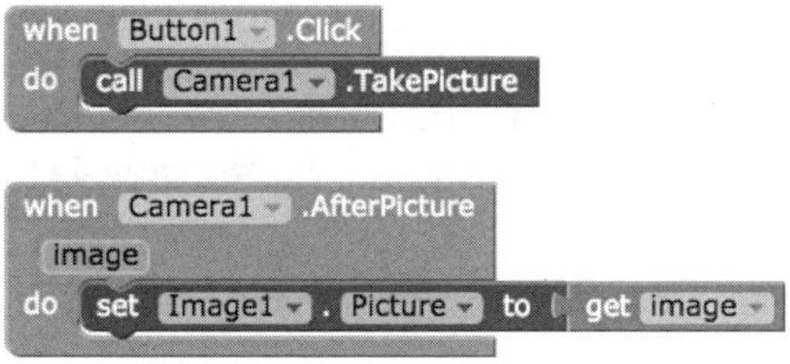

Figure 9.8 Blocks that drive a simple Camera app. When Button1 is clicked, the camera is activated. When the picture is complete, the **AfterPicture** event is triggered, where the newly created image is displayed in Image1.

The name of the new image does not have to be displayed right away. It can be saved in a variable, in a list, or in TinyDB because it is just text. But if it is not used inside the **AfterPicture** event block, the name will be lost. The picture will still exist on the phone, but you will have lost the name by which you can use it in App Inventor. The user could still find it using an ImagePicker, however. What you do with that name, as with most things in programming, depends on what you want your app to do.

Video

You can add the Video Player component from the Designer and then enable it through the Blocks Editor. When the application is run, the player shows videos in a rectangular frame inside the app.

When the user touches the video, a set of controls appears, much like the functionality of YouTube or similar video-playing apps on Android. Video files must be in specific formats, such as .wmv.

When running the applications, the video player displays in a frame onscreen. If the user touches it, controls appear, such as play/pause, skip ahead, or skip backward. The player can also be controlled with **Start**, **Pause**, or **SeekTo** blocks.

All files should be in one of the Android-supported media formats, such as .mp4 or .wmv.

App Inventor permits only files less than 1 MB and limits the total size of any application to 5 MB, so do not plan on a substantial amount of media in any application. If the files are too large, you will see errors when packaging the app for distribution. If you really want to use a certain video, it might be worth editing it down in length, resolution, and/or compression.

Another workaround is to set the media source to point to a URL that plays the video from the website. Your app can download a file from the Internet, too. See Chapter 11, "Databases," for more on how to use the Web component to do this.

A Camcorder component also works exactly like the Camera component. It launches the phone's built-in video recording app (likely the same one that the Camera component uses for still pictures) and returns with an event named AfterRecording. Inside the AfterRecording event is a parameter named **clip** that holds the name of the newly created video file. This can be used with the Video Player component or any other mechanism that uses video.

Exercise: Camera Action

The purpose of this app is to build a still and video camera. This will give you practice using these components and enable you to experiment with these and other multimedia tools.

As described previously, multimedia, in particular, lends itself to playing with the various capabilities.

1. Place the Camera and Camcorder components onto the Viewer. These are nonvisible, so the screen will remain blank.

2. Then bring in two buttons. Give the buttons a label that corresponds to their function. Name the buttons Picture and Video. Note that you cannot name either of the buttons Camera or Camcorder because you are not allowed to give a button a name that is the same as one of the components. This is one example of when leaving the component names as defaults is an acceptable practice; there will be only one of each in the entire app.

3. In the Blocks Editor, program each of the buttons to launch the camera and camcorder, respectively, when the buttons are pressed.

4. Use your phone to test the video recording and camera functionality. Be sure to test how well the existing camera and video capabilities work within the context of the app you have built.

Additional Exercises

1. Add a different multimedia element to this app. You might want to include the sound recorder or another piece, adding it to the existing options or eliminating one of the others.

2. Look for ways multimedia components could strengthen apps that you built from previous lessons or ones that you created on your own.

Summary

App Inventor offers some strong multimedia possibilities. You can add audio, video, and images to your apps to make them more engaging. This is an essential component of many apps that developers create, so having experience with this will certainly be helpful later.

Your users can select existing media with the ImagePicker and create new media with the Camera and Camcorder.

At this point, your toolkit should be fairly robust for creating many different kinds of apps. Going forward, a good learning activity is to begin creating apps outside the parameters of what you have built to this point.

Summary

10

Sensors

One of the biggest differences between mobile computing and traditional desktop computing is that the mobile device moves with the user through the different situations in life. This *situatedness* isn't just so the user can access the phone at any time; it also enables the phone to access more information about the user and the environment. Smartphones have sensors in them that can help read the world around them, which is a great data source for apps to use. One such sensor is the Location Sensor, with a GPS receiver at its core, which enables the phone to identify where it is in the world. Google Maps (see Figure 10.1) can suggest restaurants because it knows where you are. Apps might be able to combine your location data with information gathered from others and tell you which of your friends are nearby or how bad traffic is looking.

Sensors also play a critical role in games. A big part of this is the Accelerometer Sensor, which, as you might guess, measures acceleration. Over time, the accelerometer has become a critical piece of mobile gaming because it lets the player tilt and move the device for a more interactive experience. Motion sensing in all gaming platforms has an accelerometer at its heart. Modern gaming sensors also have a gyroscope sensor for more accurate motion tracking, and most newer smartphones do, too.

These and other types of sensors are important in making your app come to life. In this chapter, we explore the backgrounds of these different options and then look at an example app for how to best put them to use.

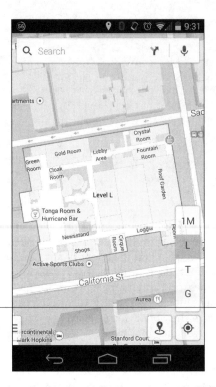

Figure 10.1   Google Maps is one of many applications that uses GPS.

Building Location-Aware Apps

The main takeaway from this chapter for you is building apps that are smarter. They will access the user's location, which enables contextual information. Next, we explore some best use cases for how to accomplish this (see Figure 10.2).

Using Location

One of the most common sensors that people use on their phones every day is GPS. The Global Positioning System uses satellites in orbit around Earth to triangulate an exact location. (That's why it is sometimes called SatNav.) This creates a variety of new use cases for different kinds of apps.

When an app can figure out its location, the door is open for many new features that use location and what's nearby as context for what the user can see and do. This is a powerful new avenue for computing, and you can probably think of a handful of apps that use location as part of their service. Some of these apps likely didn't exist yet when these words were written. Location is a powerful piece of information to have.

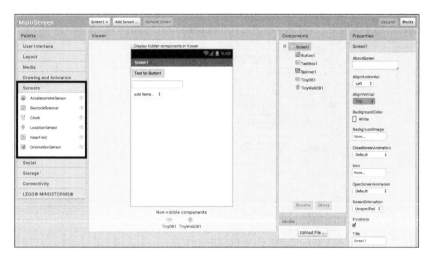

Figure 10.2   The Sensors palette in the Designer.

The Location Sensor

MIT App Inventor has the Location Sensor component for accessing location data. It has many properties, including the big three of location: latitude, longitude, and altitude (see Figure 10.3). Using a getter block on any of these properties gets the most current value of that property, as of the last time the Location Sensor updated. (If you ask for the altitude twice in a row, mere milliseconds apart, the data likely hasn't changed—or been updated—yet.)

A lot of capability is packed into this little component, so let's explore.

Notice the two event handlers: **LocationChanged** and **StatusChanged**.

An app that, say, tracks you as you go for a jog would use the **LocationChanged** event to record a new location in a list every time it changes. At the end of the jog, that list would contain the history of where you went and, potentially, at what time (if you also recorded time). You could then make maps or derive the person's speed and total time (sort of like RunKeeper and other commercial apps that track running data).

Sometimes your app cares about what kind of location data you have (including no data). Imagine that you're using a location-based app that is happily tracking your walk home, and then you go inside your house. The device might not be able to see the GPS satellites anymore, and that would trigger a **StatusChanged** event. Both **provider** and **status** are pieces of text, so you can display them and see what has changed about the status. If **status** has the piece of text *Available* in it, then you know you have a location.

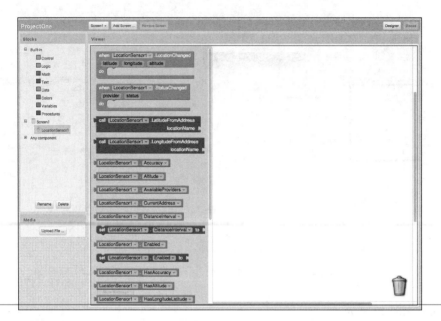

Figure 10.3   The Location Sensor blocks.

Other Location Providers

Although GPS is fairly accurate, it is not always available. Fortunately, because App Inventor was built on Android, it has some other built-in tools for tracking location.

The device can obtain a position through a wireless network. If your phone recognizes the names of nearby Wi-Fi networks, it can figure out where you are based on previous devices that have seen that named network. Cell ID also provides a location for the phone based on signals from nearby cellular towers.

The underlying Android system considers all these providers and chooses what data to use based on a constant trade-off of accuracy, speed, and battery use. You don't have to worry about this, but if you're curious, you can always query the **ProviderName** property to see where the data is currently coming from. To quote the Android developer's guide, "Obtaining user location from a mobile device can be complicated." In App Inventor, you don't have to worry about exactly where the location data came from—but you can peek, if you want.

Location Data

Location is just a set of numbers: latitude and longitude. You can always ask the Location Sensor for its most recent reading of those numbers using the getter blocks because they do appear as component properties. They're also accessible in the **LocationChanged** event as parameters. Both methods look at the same data and work exactly the same (see Figure 10.4).

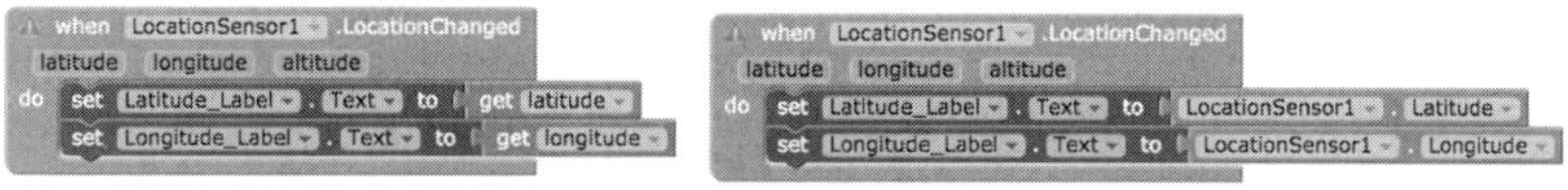

Figure 10.4   Two versions of the **LocationChanged** event: One gets the location data from the event parameters, and the other gets the data from the component properties. They work exactly the same. Only one can exist at a time in a project, however (which is why the red error stickers are present).

The blocks in Figure 10.4 represent the simplest possible GPS app: one that simply prints the latitude and longitude onto the screen. If you add one more label, you can explore a slightly more sophisticated feature. The Location Sensor looks up the nearest address of where you are simply if you ask for it, just by using the getter for **LocationSensor1.CurrentAddress**.

Note that a GPS device can take a few minutes after startup before it finds a lock on the current location. If your app asks for latitude, longitude, current address, or any other location data, App Inventor simply reports "Unavailable" (or another reasonably clear text message). You can avoid this message, however, by checking to see if the Location Sensor has found a lock, using the property **HasLongitudeLatitude**. This property returns true or false, so it is perfectly compatible with the **if** block, without needing a comparator (such as equals). You can see this in Figure 10.5. This is especially useful if you are not using the **LocationChanged** event. Perhaps your app is updating on a timer, in which case this could be a prudent precaution. **HasAccuracy** and **HasAltitude** also tell you whether the phone has either of those pieces of information. You'll more likely need these two because they don't have an event associated with them to tell you when they've been updated.

If you stick with the **LocationChanged** event, you probably won't need this.

Figure 10.5   Checking to make sure the sensor has found a lat/long lock before getting that information. If the lock has not been established, the setter blocks are skipped.

Be sure to take a look at all the blocks in the Location Sensor flyout menu—you'll find many more features than we cover in this book. More might even be added by the time you read this!

Using the Maps App with Intents

A great thing about smartphones is that you can pass off jobs to other apps on the phone. You already do this all the time. An email link opens your email app. A web link opens a web browser. A piece of location data opens a mapping app. We're going to focus on that last one.

To activate another app on an Android phone, the current app must send a special signal to the Android operating system, called an *intent*. An *intent* is a request to handle something. The operating system passes off that information to an appropriate app that knows how to handle it. If you've ever seen a dialog box pop up asking you to choose which app to use to open something, you've seen Android asking you for help in handling an intent.

Most Android phones have Google Maps installed, and that is usually the default mapping app. An intent bearing geographic data thus will be handed off to Google Maps. If you have another app that knows how to handle geographic data, you might be asked to choose which one you want to use.

To generate an intent signal, you need to have an **Activity Starter** component, which you can find in the Connectivity palette in the Designer. Drag that to your app, and it then appears in the nonvisible components area.

The **Activity Starter** needs two properties: **Action** and **DataUri**. Depending on the action, you might not need the **DataUri** property; in this example case, we do. You can set the action in the Designer or you can set it using a setter block. Either way, set the **Action** property to precisely **android.intent.action.VIEW**.

We have specified the action of the intent to be the View action. That means whatever data we give it as the **DataUri** will be viewed by an appropriate app. Let's have the intent deliver the current address of the phone. Let's create a button called **Show_Map_Button** that will trigger this. When that button is clicked, it will set up the intent and then call **StartActivity**, which will send the intent to the operating system. See Figure 10.6. *Be sure to add the* **StartActivity** *block at the end!* Setters just set data—they don't actually call anything.

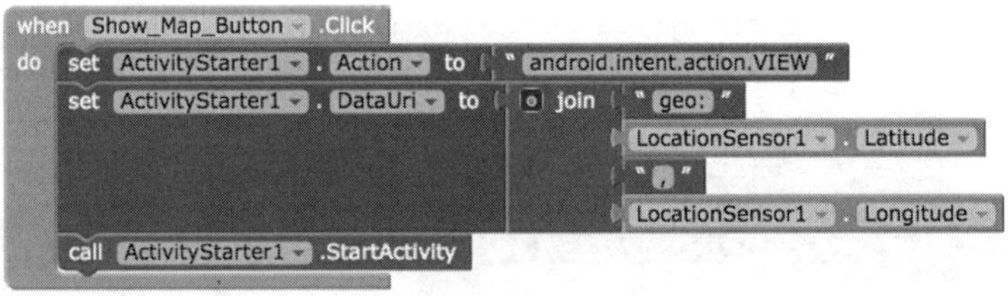

Figure 10.6   Showing your current location on a map using **Activity Starter** (which sends the location as an intent to Android).

When you are moved to the mapping app, you can return to your app by pressing Android's Back button.

If you look closely at Figure 10.6, you'll see that the **DataUri** is a single piece of text, which we build out of smaller pieces using the **join** block. The final piece of text in this example is **geo:latitude,longitude** (the words *latitude* and *longitude* were filled in with the actual data from the sensor). The **geo:** tag at the beginning is the key to being interpreted as location data. Without it, Android won't know the intended app.

The **geo:** tag supports three additional data schemes as well. (See Table 10.1 to see all of them, with code examples.) The most commonly used options in the table are the first and last, which search by coordinate and address, respectively. These are straight from the Android developer guide, so they could change. See developer.android.com/guide/components/intents-common.html.

Table 10.1 **Four Ways to Pass Location Data to the Mapping App**

Data Scheme	Description	Code Example
geo:lat,long	Shows the map at a given latitude and longitude.	join "geo:" LocationSensor1.Latitude "," LocationSensor1.Longitude
geo:lat,long?z=zoom	Similar to the previous entry, but specifies a certain zoom level. A zoom level of 1 shows the whole Earth. The closest zoom is level 23. (You probably won't need to bother with this one often.)	join "geo:" LocationSensor1.Latitude "," LocationSensor1.Longitude "?z=" 11
geo:0,0?q=lat,long(label)	Shows the given latitude and longitude, and adds a text label to that point.	join "geo:0,0?q=" LocationSensor1.Latitude "," LocationSensor1.Longitude "(My Place)"
geo:0,0?q=address	Shows the location for the given street address.	join "geo:0,0?q=" LocationSensor1.CurrentAddress

Saving Location Data

A location is just a small set of numbers, so we can save it like any other number. For example, we can store latitude and longitude in a pair of global variables. We can add them to a list. We can store them to the phone's local persistent storage with TinyDB. We can put them online with TinyWebDB. We can email them or text them, or do anything else with them, because they're just numbers.

Keep in mind that global variables, including lists stored in them, keep data only as long as the app is running. When you go back to the home screen or switch to a different application, the operating system might close your app and then data in variables would disappear. To save your data so that it reliably comes back, you have to put it somewhere persistent, such as the TinyDB. All Android apps use TinyDB for persistent storage on the device. The TinyDB database even persists when the device is restarted; it's like saving to a hard drive on a computer. Chapter 11, "Databases," discusses this in more detail.

Let's store an address in a set of global variables. This process is just as easy as setting label text in Figure 10.4 or Figure 10.5. Just for fun, here it is in Figure 10.7.

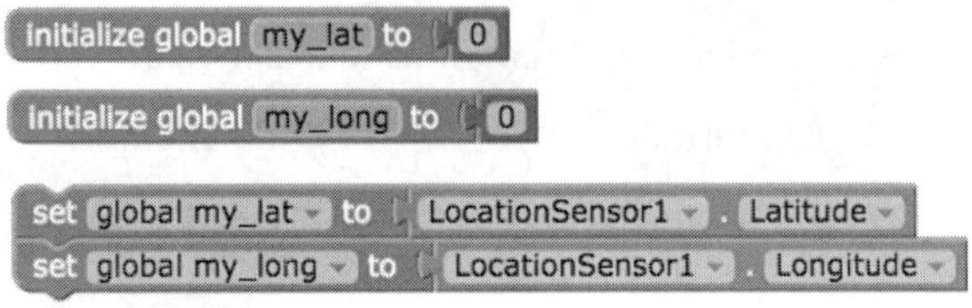

Figure 10.7   Storing the current location to global variables.

Now let's store that data so we can remember it for later, using TinyDB. Make sure you add a TinyDB component; then you can save the data (see Figure 10.8).

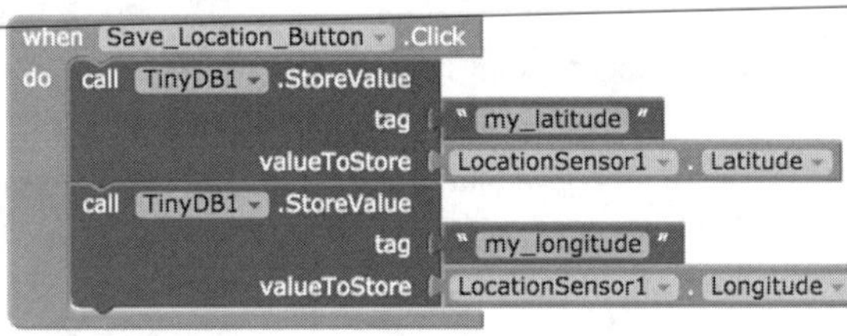

Figure 10.8   Saving current latitude and longitude to the TinyDB. This data will stay on the phone even if the app closes or the phone restarts.

Of course, storing data does us no good if we can't recall it. In the next figure, we take the data back out of TinyDB and store it in the global variables from earlier. We could just as easily put that data into labels. Figure 10.9 shows the basics of recalling the data from TinyDB. The important part here is that the tags must match exactly with the ones that were used to store the data in Figure 10.8. I used Duplicate (from the right-click menu) to make exact copies of the text blocks containing the tags.

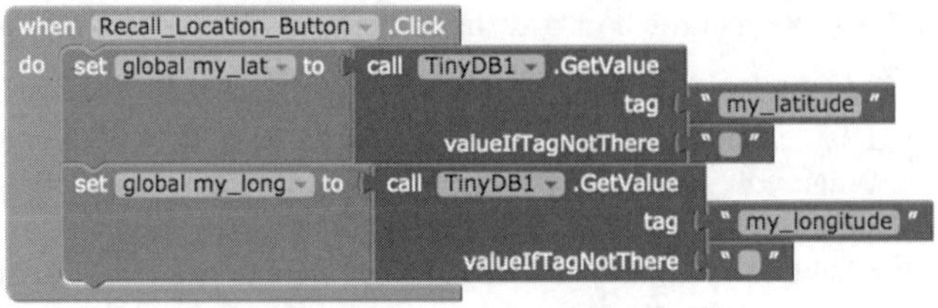

Figure 10.9   Basic recall of location data from the TinyDB.

Here we have an interesting question: What should we do if the TinyDB database has no data? The parameter **valueIfTagNotThere** is how **GetValue** tells us that it can't find the data we were asking for. If TinyDB has no data yet, such as when the user runs the app but hasn't stored anything, what do we want the variables to be set to? With the current blocks, the variables get set no matter what. In the example in Figure 10.9, if the data is missing, the variables will be set to an empty text. You can change that empty text to be anything.

What about zero? Let's think about that. A pair of zeroes is a meaningful location, Latitude 0 and Longitude 0, which describes a spot in the ocean off the coast of Africa just on the edge of the Gulf of Guinea. So maybe that's not what we want to use as our "no data found" value.

This becomes a design question. How do you want to handle this edge case? Your app will probably work fine as long as the user always saves before recalling, but how do you guarantee that? What if your app loads the stored data on initialization?

If you want just the basics of how to use sensors, you can skip ahead to the next section now.

Here's one solution for checking the data (see Figure 10.10). The goal of these blocks is to check whether the data was found and update the global variables only if we know there is real data to put in them. This is not the only solution, however—this is just one way to handle the situation, and it deals with it in a specific way that might not always be appropriate. This solution is not obvious and took some trial and error to design.

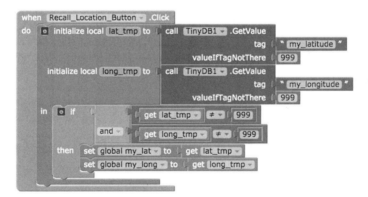

Figure 10.10   The global variables are updated to the data from TinyDB only if the data was found in TinyDB. If the data was not found, the global variables **my_lat** and **my_long** are not changed.

In Figure 10.10, the data is not stored directly in the global variables, as before; instead, it is stored in two new local variables. **valueIfTagNotThere** has been changed to the number 999. We chose this value because it doesn't make sense as either latitude or longitude. Latitude ranges from –90 to 90, and longitude ranges from –180 to 180. In both cases, 999 is out of range, so there's no way the Location Sensor will create that value. That value is now our sentinel value, which is a special value we can detect that means something. In this case, it means that the data isn't present and should not be used.

The next step is to check whether the temporary variables contain the sentinel value of 999. If neither does, then their data must be real GPS coordinates and that data is set into the globals **my_lat** and **my_long**. If either of the local variables equals 999, the set global blocks are skipped and the global variables are not updated.

This example is included more as a lesson in design than as a usable code excerpt. As your apps evolve, you will find weird corners that you need to figure out. This is one solution to one corner. Keep trying!

The Accelerometer

Smartphones have a device known as an accelerometer that measures the acceleration being applied to the phone. Acceleration is a great way to measure movement. If you shake the phone, you are accelerating it vigorously and rapidly—the accelerometer can easily detect that.

The accelerometer can also detect more subtle accelerations, which are frequently used in games. Users often can tilt or move their devices to impact game play. For example, users might have to navigate a spaceship by physically moving the device to fly in a particular direction.

This type of gaming has become popular in smartphones and helps distinguish their particular hardware capabilities from other types of gaming. If you can learn how to build this capability into your app, it will have an extra piece of sophistication to distinguish it from others. Figure 10.11 shows the Accelerometer Sensor's blocks.

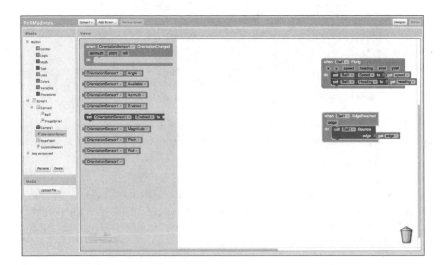

Figure 10.11   The Accelerometer Sensor blocks.

Detecting Tilt (and a Little Background Physics)

The accelerometer can detect very subtle accelerations in three directions. One such acceleration is the constant one from gravity. Think back to your physics class (or think forward if you haven't gotten there yet): Gravity constantly applies a downward acceleration to every object on Earth, even if that object is sitting completely still. If that object happens to have a three-axis accelerometer, as smartphones do, that device can detect that acceleration.

Take a look at Figure 10.12. On the left is a phone lying flat on a table, not moving. The only acceleration present is gravity, which is pulling straight down (the green arrow). The blue axes in the middle show the direction of the accelerometer's three directions of sensitivity: x, y, and z. Because the only acceleration present is in the up/down direction, it will be read on the z-axis. If the phone were moved left or right, it would be read on the x-axis. If the phone were slid forward on the table, it would be read on the y-axis.

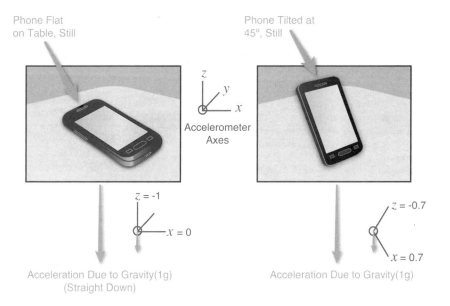

Figure 10.12   How gravity is used to detect tilting with a three-axis accelerometer.

If you tilt the phone up at 45 degrees, gravity doesn't change direction, but the phone's sensors do. Now, instead of being directly in line with the z-axis sensor, the pull of gravity is split between the z-axis and the x-axis, as shown on the right side of the figure. As a result of this tilt, the phone reads a lower value on both the x-axis and the z-axis. How *much* lower depends on how far the tilt is. The less tilt, the closer to 0 x will be and the closer to 1 z will be.

If we wanted an app that detected right/left tilt, we could just look at the x-axis and know that zero means perfectly flat, negative means tilting one way, and positive means tilting the other way.

Another way to detect tilt is to use the Orientation Sensor, which the following section discusses. The Orientation Sensor gives a direct reading of tilt and angle, which, depending on your application, might be more useful than the Acceleration Sensor.

The Orientation Sensor

Nearly every Android device supports the useful Acceleration Sensor, but another sensor also gives you physical information. The Orientation Sensor tells how the phone is oriented relative to the Earth. This sensor provides roll, pitch, and azimuth data.

Imagine for a moment that the phone is an airplane (Figure 10.13). Looking at the phone as you normally would, the top (earpiece) would be the nose of the plane and the bottom (the home button and so on) would be the tail end. The roll is how much the plane rotates without the tail or nose moving, or how much the wings move up and down. The pitch is how much higher or lower the nose is than the tail.

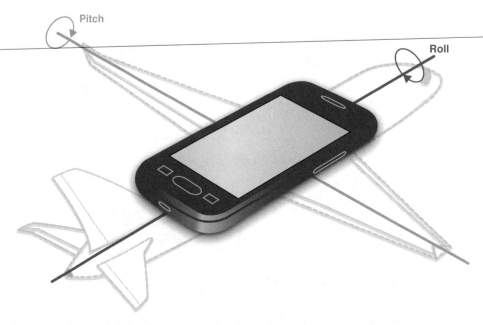

Figure 10.13   Imagine that the phone is an airplane—the pitch and roll data provided by the Orientation Sensor now make more sense.

The azimuth tells how the phone is pointed relative to magnetic north, effectively making it a compass reading. Most phones have a devoted compass-like sensor built in, which is probably where this reading comes from. But not all phones do, so do not be surprised if this feature doesn't work well on every device. Figure 10.14 shows the Orientation Sensor blocks.

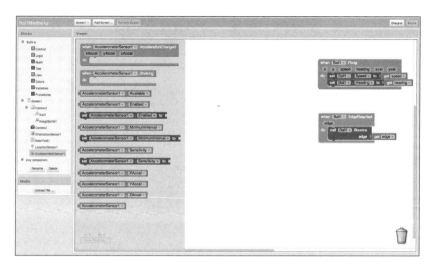

Figure 10.14   The Orientation Sensor blocks.

Unlike the accelerometer, which can use acceleration data to approximate tilt, the Orientation Sensor tries to give you a direct reading of tilt and direction.

Exercise: Pushpin

The Pushpin app does two things. First, it provides a readout of current location data, including latitude, longitude, and address. You can use it just to figure out where you are. The second thing it does is remember a location. Wherever you are, you can touch the Pin button, and it will pin your current location (which just means that it saves it). You can view the current location or the pinned location in a map application. Figure 10.15 shows the finished app.

This app has a lot of components, but they're not difficult. The GPS readout has numerous parts, all of which are labels that display a specific piece of data. The functionality is actually simple.

Make sure you drag in an **Activity Starter**; you'll need that later.

Part 1: Designing Current Location Readout

The top half of the Pushpin app is simply a readout of the current location, as reported by the Location Sensor. It has fields to display most of the data that the Location Sensor provides. The colored boxes are special labels that start off pink and turn blue when a GPS lock is made. We will create this feature in the blocks that follow.

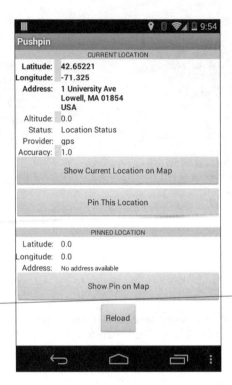

Figure 10.15   The completed Pushpin app in use.

The Current Location section of the app is one large Table Arrangement component (found in the Layout palette). This Table Arrangement has three columns and seven rows. The first column is labels that don't change—Latitude:, Longitude:, and so on. The third column contains labels that will change to show the current location data. Between them, the second column is used for small labels that we will use as a color indicator to show when a lock is made. Those "lights" are just labels with no text that have a fixed pixel width and a background color.

When the app first starts, the color indicator labels (lights) are pink (see Figure 10.16); they turn blue when a lock is made (refer back to Figure 10.15 for an example).

When an accuracy measurement is available, the light on the Accuracy row turns from pink to blue. If the measurement is ever lost, it turns back to pink. We will build this trick later. For now, let's set up the screen in the Designer. Right now, we focus only on the Current Location section of the app, which is the top half. In the Designer, that half looks like Figure 10.17.

Drag in a Label to make the CURRENT LOCATION heading. Below it, add a **TableArrangement**. Below that, add a button.

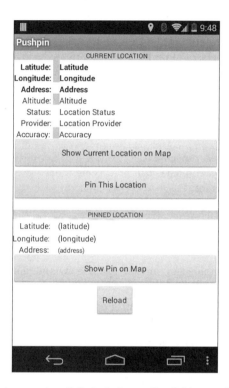

Figure 10.16   The Pushpin app when it first starts up. The lights are pink, to indicate that a lock has not yet been made for those pieces of data.

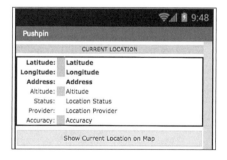

Figure 10.17   The Current Location part of the Pushpin app, as seen in the Designer. This uses a **TableArrangement**.

To make the heading label look snappy, I changed the font size to 10, the background color to Light Gray, the width to Fill Parent, and the text alignment to Center.

Rename the button to **Show_Current_Map_Button** to reflect its purpose: to show the current location on the map. Update the text to match, and set the font size to 12. You can also set the font alignment to Center and set the width to Fill Parent.

I won't mention setting font centering and width to Fill Parent for the rest of the app; if you see that the component is wide and centered, go ahead and do it.

Also, I changed the **AlignHorizontal** property of Screen1 to be **Center**, which makes centering more convenient.

Now let's deal with the **TableArrangement**. I renamed it to **CurrentTableArrangement** because it contains all the current location data. This arrangement has three columns and seven rows, and its width is set to Fill Parent.

All the components in this **TableArrangement** are labels. Table 10.2 describes which labels go where and tells what they do. All labels have a font size of 12. The location in the table corresponds to the location in the **TableArrangement**. Blank cells have no components in them.

Table 10.2   **Setting All the Labels in the TableArrangement to Display Current Location**

Text: **Latitude:**	Text: None (empty)	Text: **Latitude**
(Doesn't change; has a space at the end)	Name: *Has_Latitude*	(Text doesn't matter; will be updated)
Name: *LabelLat*	Background Color Pink	Name: *Latitude_Label*
FontBold TextAlign right	Width 10 pixels	FontBold TextAlign left
	Height Fill Parent	
Text: **Longitude:**	Text: None (empty)	Text: **Longitude**
(Doesn't change; has a space at the end)	Name: *Has_Longitude*	(Text doesn't matter; will be updated)
Name: *LabelLong*	Background Color Pink	Name: *Longitude_Label*
FontBold TextAlign right	Width 10 pixels	FontBold TextAlign left
	Height Fill Parent	
Text: **Address:**		Text: **Address**
(Doesn't change; has a space at the end)		(Text doesn't matter; will be updated)
Name: *LabelAddr*		Name: *Address_Label*
FontBold TextAlign right		FontBold TextAlign left
Text: Altitude:	Text: None (empty)	Text: Altitude
(Doesn't change; has a space at the end)	Name: *Has_Altitude*	(Text doesn't matter; will be updated)
Name: *LabelAlt*	Background Color Pink	Name: *Altitude_Label*
TextAlign right	Width 10 pixels	TextAlign left
	Height Fill Parent	

Text: Status:		Text: Location Status
(Doesn't change; has a space at the end)		(Text doesn't matter; will be updated)
Name: *LabelStat*		Name: *Location_Status_Label*
TextAlign right		TextAlign left
Text: Provider:		Text: Location Provider
(Doesn't change; has a space at the end)		(Text doesn't matter; will be updated)
Name: *LabelProv*		Name: *Location_Provider_ Label*
TextAlign right		TextAlign left
Text: Accuracy:	Text: None (empty)	Text: Accuracy
(Doesn't change; has a space at the end)	Name: *Has_Accuracy*	(Text doesn't matter; will be updated)
Name: *LabelProv*	Background Color Pink	Name: *Location_Accuracy_ Label*
TextAlign right	Width 10 pixels	TextAlign left
	Height Fill Parent	

Programming Part 1: The Current Location Readout

Updating all those labels from Part 1 takes some work to set up. Let's start with the easy ones: the data fields. Each label in the right column simply needs to be filled with the corresponding property of the Location Sensor, as in Figure 10.18. Assemble these blocks, but don't put them anywhere yet—we have more to make.

Figure 10.18   Setting the data field labels to their corresponding data from the Location Sensor.

Notice the pink **trim** block in Figure 10.18. I added that later while designing the app because the **CurrentAddress** feature tends to add extra empty lines after the address. Those extra lines aren't necessary in our display, so **trim**, found in the text built-in menu, cuts them out. Trim removes all extra white space, including new lines, spaces, and tabs.

Next, let's make those colored lights work to indicate whether we have a lock. The **LocationSensor** has three tests that provide this information: **HasLongitudeLatitude**, **HasAltitude**, and **HasAccuracy**. Those three getters respond with a value of true or false, which answers the question and is the right format to give to an **if** block (see Figure 10.19).

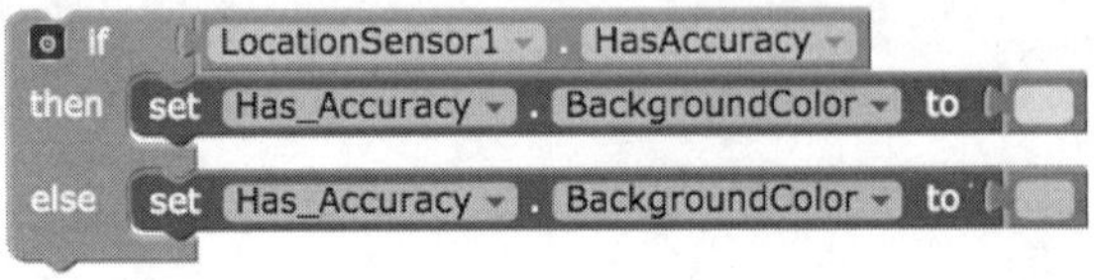

Figure 10.19   Asking the Location Sensor about **HasAccuracy**, which reports true or false directly. The color of the light is set to blue if the Location Sensor has a lock and pink if it does not.

If accuracy has been acquired, **HasAccuracy** reports **true** and the first setter in the **then** section runs, setting the color to blue. If it reports **false**, the first setter is skipped and the blocks in the **else** section run instead, setting the color to pink.

We simply repeat this logic for all three sets of "has" tests (see Figure 10.20).

Figure 10.20   Checking the availability of all three data points and updating the colors of the lights accordingly. Latitude and longitude share one test but have two different lights to update.

Now let's combine the label updates and the data availability updates. We will want to run this big stack of blocks more than once, so let's make a procedure to put it in. Drag out an empty **procedure** block from the Procedures built-in menu, rename it **update_location_data**, and drag in the blocks we've just assembled, as in Figure 10.21. This procedure will update all our data elements in the current location readout whenever it is called.

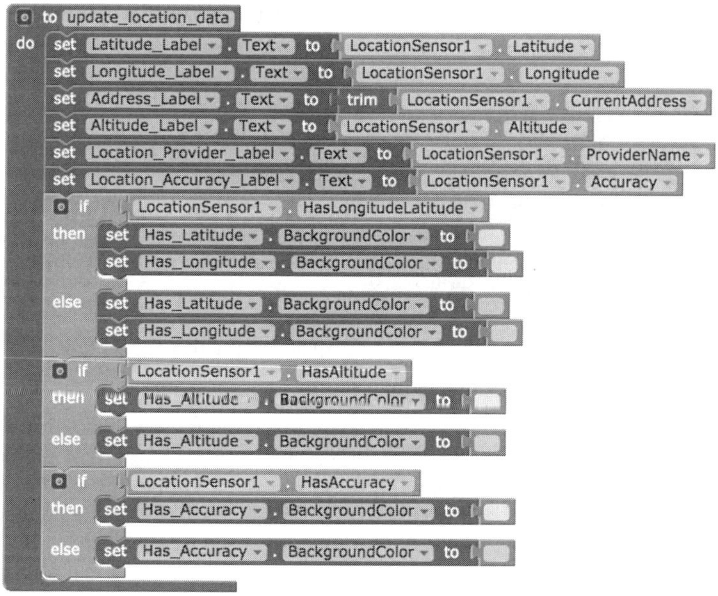

Figure 10.21   Connect the previously assembled blocks and insert them into a new procedure definition, which you should rename to **update_location_data**.

Two events let us know when something in that readout has changed: **LocationChanged** and **StatusChanged**. Both of these should call the procedure we just made. Additionally, the **StatusChanged** event updates the **Location_Status_Label** because the only time the status is available is inside that event. Figure 10.22 shows both events.

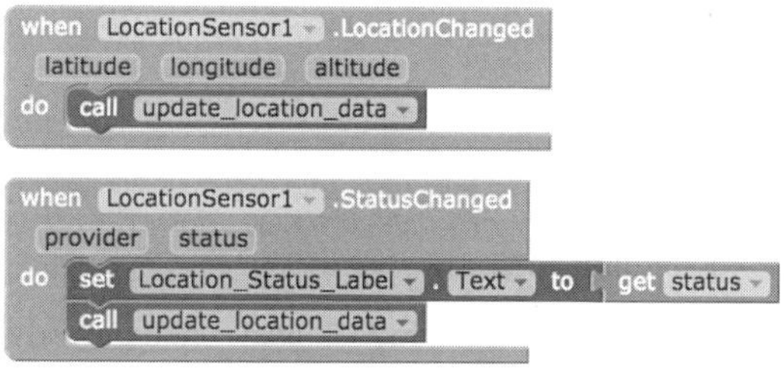

Figure 10.22   The two events that trigger updates to the current location display: **LocationChanged** and **StatusChanged**. Both call the **update_location_data** procedure, which updates the display.

All that's left for this section is the button to show the current location on the map. That works exactly as shown earlier in this chapter. When that button is clicked, we want to hand off the current location (as displayed in the labels) to the mapping app through the **Activity Starter** (see Figure 10.23).

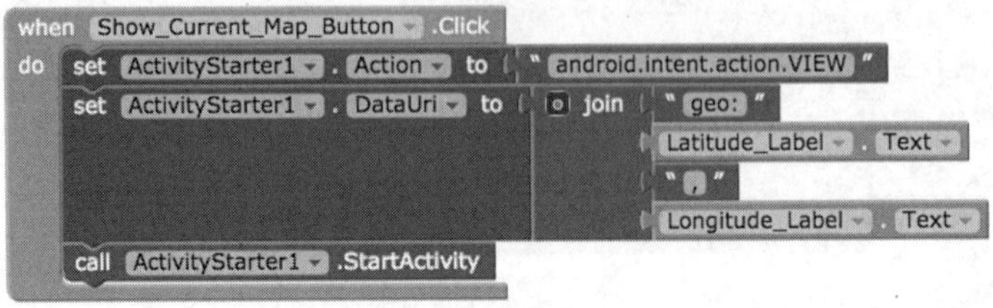

Figure 10.23   Showing the current location in a mapping app using the **Activity Starter**.

The first part of this app is done, so feel free to try it. (You might have to go outside.) If all you need is an app that tells you the current location, you can consider it done. One more part remains now for this chapter—we will pin a location for recalling later.

Part 2: Pinning a Location to Remember Later

We have completed the top half of the app, which shows the current location data and lets you view that location on a map. Next, we add the capability to save the current location. We're using the word *pin* to describe saving a location for later.

Picking up from Part 1, we have some more components to add. Figure 10.24 shows the entire app in the Designer.

Add a button with the text Pin This Location. Name it **Pin_Location_Button**. Below that is a spacer label, which has no text or color but has a height of 12 pixels. This is just to create some space on the screen.

Below the spacer, add a heading label like the one at the top of the screen that reads PINNED LOCATION.

Below it, add another **TableArrangement**. Below that, add a button with the text Show Pin on Map. Name that button (as you might guess) **Show_Pinned_Map_Button.**

There's one more button to add, but we'll toss that in at the very end.

This **TableArrangement**, which I renamed **PinnedTableArrangement**, has three rows and three columns. Table 10.3 shows what components should be in that **TableArrangement**. All the labels use size 12 font, except where noted. Cells in this table correspond to the cells of the **TableArrangement**. Blank cells have no components in them.

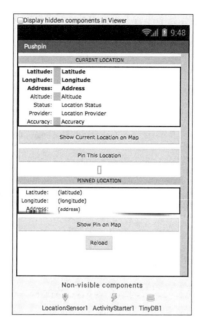

Figure 10.24   The entire Pushpin app in the Designer. Note the empty label used as a spacer in the middle (highlighted in green).

Table 10.3   **All the Labels in the TableArrangement to Display the Pinned Location**

Text: Latitude:	Text: none	Text: (latitude)
(Doesn't change; has a space at the end)	Name: **Spacer_Label2**	(Text doesn't matter; will be updated)
Name: **LabelPinLat**	No text. Width 10 pixels.	Name: **Pinned_Latitude_Label**
TextAlign right		TextAlign left.
Text: Longitude:		Text: (longitude)
(Doesn't change; has a space at the end)		(Text doesn't matter; will be updated)
Name: **LabelPinLong**		Name: **Pinned_Longitude_Label**
TextAlign right		TextAlign left
Text: Address:		Text: (address)
(Doesn't change; has a space at the end)		(Text doesn't matter; will be updated)
Name: **LabelPinAddr**		Name: **Pinned_Address_Label**
TextAlign right		TextAlign left. Font size 10

Programming Part 2: Pinning a Location

This part of the app is actually easier to program than Part 1 because fewer elements are involved. Let's start by creating the core feature: pinning a location. When the **Pin_Location_Button** is clicked, we want to do two things: copy the Current Location text to the Pinned Location display and save it in TinyDB.

Drag a TinyDB component into the Designer, if you have not already done so.

Assemble the click event handler for the **Pin_Location_Button** (see Figure 10.25).

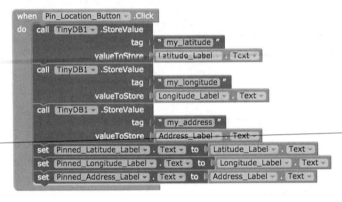

Figure 10.25   When the **Pin_Location_Button** is clicked, store the current location data to the TinyDB and copy it to the Pinned Location display.

We can now save and update the pinned location. Next, let's hook up the button to show the pinned location on a map. We'll use the same **Activity Starter** code as the Current Location button, so you can duplicate that handler and modify it to avoid assembling the whole thing from scratch. When completed, it should look like Figure 10.26.

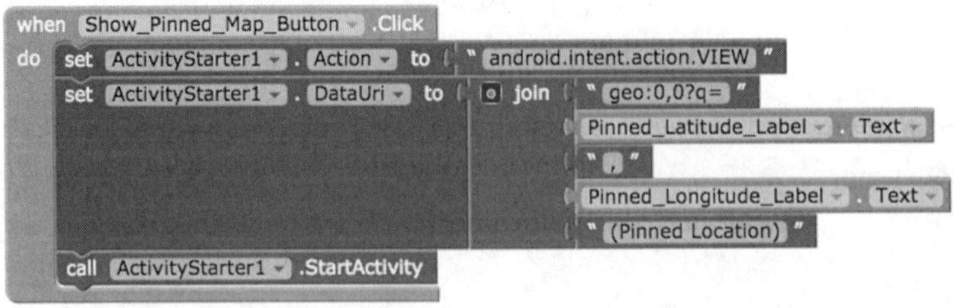

Figure 10.26   When the button is clicked to show the pinned location on the map, set up the **Activity Starter** to display the pinned location and then launch it. This uses a slightly different format for the **DataUri** to add a label to the map that reads Pinned Location.

We're almost there! All that remains is the Reload button, which will reload all the data and retrieve the pinned location from the TinyDB.

Add a button to the bottom of the app in the Designer. Name it **ReloadButton**. Set its text to Reload. Then jump back to the blocks page.

The Reload button needs to do two things when it is clicked. First, it must run the **update_location_data** procedure we used earlier. That necessitates the call block for the existing procedure—nothing more. Then this event needs to retrieve the pinned location data from the TinyDB and set that information into the Pinned readout. I used the method from earlier in the chapter to make sure the data was in the TinyDB. If nothing was saved, it will not update the Pinned display (see Figure 10.27).

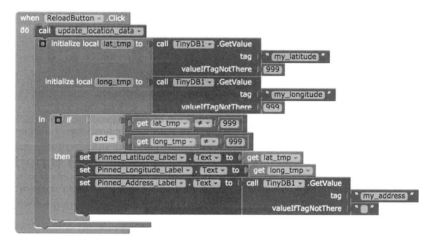

Figure 10.27   The Reload button does two things: calls the **update_location_data** procedure and restores the Pinned Location information from the TinyDB. In this figure, it checks the TinyDB data before setting it to the display, which is explained earlier in the chapter.

When the app first starts up, it is empty (see Figure 10.16). When it gets location data, it updates the display (see Figure 10.15). When you press the Pin This Location button, it copies the location from Current Location into Pinned Location and saves it persistently in the TinyDB. Pressing Reload restores a previously saved Pinned Location and updates the Current Location display.

Try it out!

Extension Activities

- Use lists to extend the Pushpin app to save more than one pinned location. Save as many as you like.

- Transform Pushpin into a new app so that two friends can exchange their locations using TinyWebDB.

- Add sound effects to inform the user when updates are received (this one is easy).

Summary

Sensors play an important part in app development because they allow the device to interact with location and data. Using sensors opens up many different opportunities in the kind of apps you can build and how they function.

The Location Sensor gives you the power of the GPS chip and other location data, which can be used, saved, and displayed. Visualizing a point on a map is easy using the **Activity Starter**.

The Accelerometer Sensor measures acceleration from motion and gravity and can be used to detect shaking as well as specific motions. It can approximate tilt because gravity is always accelerating the device (and everything else) downward.

The Orientation Sensor gives direct access to the phone's understanding of tilt, on two axes (pitch and roll), and reads what compass direction the phone is pointing.

Using sensors effectively requires some more thought and planning than other elements. Location opens up a larger world of data and information that can make the app a powerful, interactive experience. It creates more options with mapping, games, social media, and more. Maybe you'll think of a new use!

Databases

Much of the discussion surrounding mobile apps and consumer technology in general focuses on data. Almost every app that you use collects some form of user data, which is typically necessary for the service to be effective. Think about the apps you use most commonly. Facebook? Twitter? Most of them are just tools that connect you to a source of data.

Creating and maintaining such databases is a tremendous task and typically can take a lot of resources from a company. For example, the company Nutritionix builds and maintains an online database of food information, such as ingredients lists and nutritional information. This company doesn't make a single app; it only provides a mechanism for others to use its data. The point is, data is a really big deal.

Fortunately, you can get a taste of working with data with little difficulty.

A database is not just a giant storehouse of online information. Databases are *persistent*, meaning that their data survives even when the app is closed. All the variables and lists that we have used so far are not persistent. When the app is closed, that data can be lost and reset unless it is saved somewhere persistently.

App Inventor does much of the work when it comes to accessing data through a database. You have the capability to create apps that store the data on an Android device or share it with other devices.

In this chapter, we look at the two ways App Inventor manages database information: with TinyDB and TinyWebDB. The former stores data on an Android device, which is preferable for apps that need to quickly access information or apps that do not require being shared with others (and apps that are not sensitive from a security standpoint). TinyWebDB is preferable for apps that share information among devices.

Two more advanced database features come into play as well. Google FusionTables is a service that enables sophisticated data storage and retrieval. App Inventor can also interact with web servers and web services using the Web component.

TinyDB

As previously mentioned, two components are used to manage databases: TinyDB and TinyWebDB. TinyDB is used to store persistent data on the Android device itself. This is important for apps when the user has no need to share the data with another person or device (and the data presents no security risk).

Both TinyDB and TinyWebDB are found in the Blocks Editor with the other storage components (see Figure 11.1).

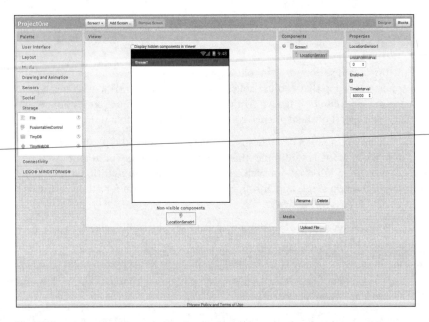

Figure 11.1   Storage components in the Designer.

With TinyDB, the data is stored directly on the device and is available for your app. For example, if you program an app to provide an automatic response to a button press or some other command, the response is stored in a database. It is then retrieved every time the user requests it.

The Blocks Editor has several programming options for storing and then calling the data when needed (see Figure 11.2).

You can see that you have many different choices for using data. Databases in App Inventor always use a tag-value pair. The tag identifies the data for later retrieval.

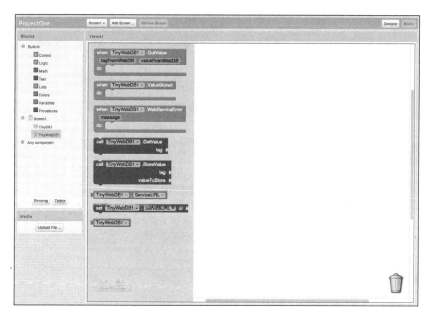

Figure 11.2   The TinyDB blocks.

Retrieving Data from TinyDB

Getting data from the database is accomplished with the **TinyDB.GetValue** block. The following example illustrates triggering a response when the user pushes a button. For this use case, we want this data always and rapidly available (see Figure 11.3).

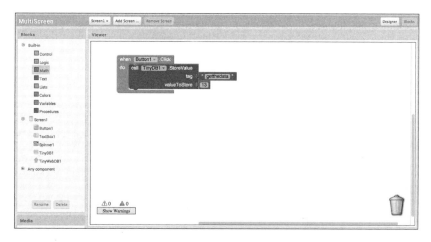

Figure 11.3   Programming a button to store the value with the tag **getthedata** in TinyDB.

A Few TinyDB Details

A note on TinyDB: There's only one. Adding more than one TinyDB component does nothing. More components, with different names, all attach to the same database in Android, so more than one is redundant and unnecessary. If you store a value with one TinyDB, all the others will be able to retrieve it. Just use a single TinyDB component per app. If you want to use multiple TinyDB components to organize your data, then use different tags or tag prefixes (for example, use **Set1_name** and **Set2_name** as the tags).

Each app has a separate TinyDB storage location on the device, so apps will never cross data. It is impossible for one app to read the data of another's TinyDB. However, if you are running in Live Mode with the Companion app, the Companion app itself only has one database, and that may persist into you loading a new app in App Inventor to work on. This bleedover will not happen after the app is built and installed, so it is usually not a problem. The TinyDB component does have blocks to retrieve the tags in the database and to clear the whole database, and you can use them if you are unsure of the state of the database.

TinyWebDB

As discussed earlier, TinyWebDB stores data by using a web-based database. By default, the component accesses a shared database run by the App Inventor team: http://appinvtinywebdb. appspot.com.

This is a demonstration web service: The App Inventor team warns that it could go offline as it is being modified and also cautions that it has very limited storage space—your app's data could get bumped if another app takes up residence and demands more space.

Despite this caveat, it should function well for those who are looking to first dabble with a database. In most cases, the data should be fine and should work without any major issues, especially if you are using just a small amount while building or testing an app. However, anyone looking to deploy an app with App Inventor will want a more reliable and stable solution.

Setting Up Your Own Web Database Service

App Inventor provides a step-by-step tutorial on creating a custom web service with Google App Engine at http://appinventor.mit.edu/explore/ai2/custom-tinywebdb.html.

After following the tutorial, you won't have to depend on the shared default database, which all of the App Inventor world uses. With your own TinyWebDB service, nobody but you will be using the service, so you don't have to worry about others bumping your data out or overwriting your tags.

Security and Privacy

TinyWebDB is inherently insecure. It does not require a password to access, which means that anyone in the world can access it. This is a *feature*, in that it is easy to get a demonstration app running with a simple shared database. However, any data that you put in a TinyWebDB—even if you create your own service—can possibly be read by anyone. *Do not put any sensitive information into TinyWebDB, even for a moment.* Data that is not "sensitive" is data that you—and your users—wouldn't mind seeing printed on a billboard by the highway. Anything in TinyWebDB is potentially public. Additionally, anyone can call the **erase** command in TinyWebDB because that command does not require a password, either. *Do not use TinyWebDB for data that needs to be stored for a long time.* If you need secure, hardy storage, either keep the data on the device with TinyWebDB (assuming, of course, that you will not lose your phone) or use a more sophisticated database solution such as FusionTables.

FusionTables

FusionTables is a Google product that works like an online spreadsheet but enables you to access the data directly from your app and make structured queries. The query mechanism is a professional-strength feature, so you can ask for specific parts of the data. For instance, a query lets you ask for all the people who are registered for a certain class. The previous database systems in this chapter are easier but less powerful, so you'd have to create that sort of organization yourself.

FusionTables can handle a huge amount of data, far more than TinyWebDB. It is also private and secure, unlike TinyWebDB. It lets you make specific queries, including adding and modifying data, thus giving you a great deal of control over your large data stores. It is a great tool for an app that will handle more than a "small" amount of data.

App Inventor provides a **FusionTablesControl** component, which provides blocks for the most-used features of FusionTables.

The **FusionTablesControl** component is in the Storage drawer in the Designer. If you click the question mark next to it in the palette, you bring up a long introduction pop-up (see Figure 11.4). That pop-up explains the basics of how to get started with FusionTables, and you should read, understand, and follow those instructions before you try to use the component.

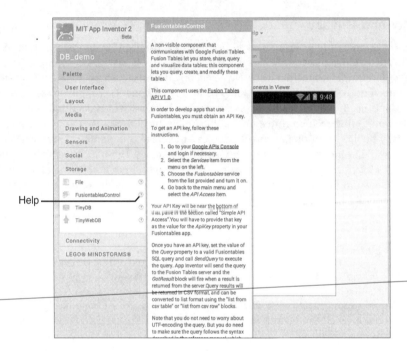

Figure 11.4   This introduction to FusionTables appears when you click the Help question mark in the Designer.

Clicking the More Information link at the bottom of the info pop-up brings you to the documentation page for the **FusionTablesControl**. That page also has key information for getting set up with FusionTables—see this URL:

http://ai2.appinventor.mit.edu/reference/components/storage.html#FusiontablesControl

Figure 11.5 shows the important blocks in using **FusionTables**:

- **Set ApiKey**—Use this to set the API key you got from the Google console. This needs to be set only once (if you are using only one table). This block is not necessary if the **ApiKey** is set in the Designer.

- **Set Query**—Use this to set the query that will be sent to FusionTables. Writing good and valid queries is the heart of FusionTables. The full query language is explained in the Google Developers' documentation, and some formats from that documentation are included below.

- **Call SendQuery**—This procedure block sends the query to FusionTables for processing. Make sure the **ApiKey** and **Query** properties are set before calling this procedure. This block simply sends the request; the response triggers a **GotResult** event.

- **When GotResult (result)**—This event is triggered when the device receives a response from a FusionTables query. The result of the query is in the "result" parameter. This result is in CSV format, so you'll need one of the "list from CSV" blocks to convert it to a usable App Inventor list. The data will be either a row (a single list) or a table (a list containing rows, where each row is another list), depending on what the query requested.

Figure 11.5   Important blocks for using FusionTables. Included are two blue blocks from the Lists palette, which translate the result data into ordinary App Inventor lists.

FusionTables are their own product, separate from App Inventor. Take the time to learn how they work. Understand that the features could change independently of App Inventor, so always check with the Google Developers site on FusionTables to stay up-to-date. That page is linked from all the App Inventor help pages and is shown here:

https://developers.google.com/fusiontables/docs/v1/getting_started

Writing queries is the trickiest and most important part of using FusionTables. No single right answer for queries exists. Instead, your query depends on the setup of your table, what data is in the table, and what you want to do with that data. Table 11.1 has some query formats taken from the Google Developers site, to give you an idea of what a query looks like. The versions we have in this excerpt are formatted to fit in the **Query** property of the **FusionTablesControl** component. All queries are a single line of text.

Table 11.1   **Key Query Formats for FusionTables**

Query Action	Query Format
Lists all rows within a table.	SELECT ROWID FROM <table_id>
Gets a specific row. See the Google developer documentation for what filters are possible.	SELECT ROWID FROM <table_id> WHERE <your filter>
Inserts a new row into a table. The column names and values must be comma separated, and the order of names and values must match.	INSERT INTO <table_id> (<column_names>) VALUES (<values>)
Updates a specific row. Multiple **<column name> = <value>** pairs can be specified, separated by commas.	UPDATE <table_id> SET <column_name> = <value> WHERE ROWID = <row_id>
Deletes a specific row.	DELETE FROM <table_id> {WHERE ROWID = <row_id>}

You can also access Google's FusionTables using a **GET** request, which the next section explains. All of the FusionTablesControl blocks are actually making **GET** and **POST** requests behind the scenes, so you can re-create their features with the **GET** and **POST** blocks of the Web component. Generally, you don't need to do this unless you want to use more complex features of FusionTables that the built-in component does not have.

FusionTables is possibly the easiest way to get the power of a relational database in your app. However, it is not strictly *easy*. Learning and appreciating what the FusionTables service is and how it works will take time. Plan for this time, and soon you'll be able to create high-end data processing apps.

Using Web **GET** and **POST**

The Web component, under the Connectivity palette in the Designer, offers one more way to interact with data over the Internet and get access to public databases. The Web component provides direct access to the most low-level tool that any web browser has, which is to request a page from somewhere on the Internet by URL. The Web component also has the capability to post text or a file to a web server. With those two capabilities, you can communicate with basic web servers around the world.

Any response you get using the Web component can be delivered to you in the blocks or saved as a file. If the **SaveResponse** property is checked or set to true, it saves the response as a file and gives you the name of the file as a response event parameter. For the rest of the section, you can assume that **SaveResponse** is off, so the text response will be handled just as text.

Basic Files

You can store data on a server somewhere and then pull it directly into your app. This lets you update the data without having to update the app. It can even happen every time the app launches and be invisible "magic" to your users.

Consider this simple app as an example. When the button is clicked, it fetches the file (specified in the blocks) and displays that file in the label. Figure 11.6 shows such a design, and Figure 11.7 shows the simple blocks that use the Web component to fetch the file from the Internet.

Figure 11.6   Design of a demo app that fetches text from a website on the Internet.

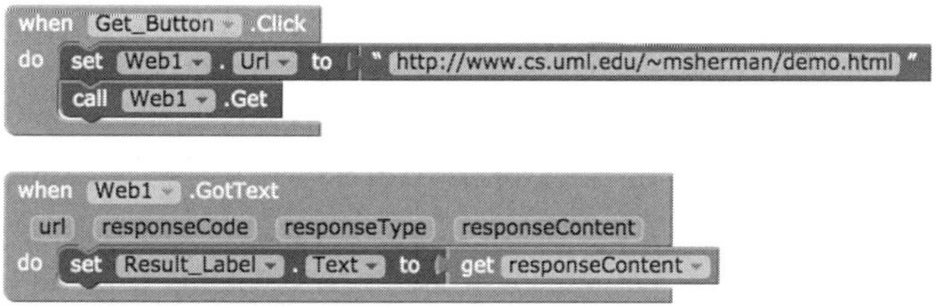

Figure 11.7   Blocks that use a **Get** request to fetch a particular file from the Web. The content of that file is displayed in the **Result_Label**.

This app just puts the text in the label, so you're likely to see a lot of messy HTML code. It is a web page, so it is intended to be read by a browser, not as plain text.

You can use this trick to store a data file on a website somewhere (as long as it has a direct URL) and have your app grab that file. Then you can update that file whenever you want on the website, and the app will get the latest data without having to do an update through the Play Store.

One example is an app that helps you judge character mappings in a video game. The app is just the processor; the actual data about which characters possess what properties is stored as a text file online. You can use this technique to download the file and then use the blocks in the built-in Text palette to parse it.

Web APIs

Many services on the Web provide an API (application programming interface) to enable developers like you to access their service and the data within it. The details of how web service APIs work is beyond the scope of this book, but here are the pieces you need to get App Inventor to work with them.

App Inventor can use any RESTful web API that makes and accepts http **GET**, **POST**, and **PUT** requests. It can post files (including images and video) and also receive both files and text.

The key is, it cannot do anything beyond stateless, individual requests. It cannot provide payload data—the entire request must be in the URL. It cannot use an API that depends on a prolonged session or connection. This could change in the future, but the Web component is currently limited in this way.

You can use pretty much any API you find that works by constructing a URL, without the need for payload data.

Exercise: WriteMore

The following app is a shared writing activity that can be fun with a group of friends. You might have been part of a classroom exercise in which one person starts with a word and then others keep adding their own words or sentences. The story takes on a life of its own, and everyone has a good laugh over how wacky it comes out.

Using shared data, we can create that kind of experience on an Android device. This next app, which we call WriteMore, could function as a fun party game or just as a good way to show off what App Inventor is capable of.

The app uses many of the same principles discussed in this chapter, such as storing and retrieving data from TinyWebDB.

The database storage will be put to use holding on to words that you type and submit in the app. Then another user can add a word, which will be saved in the database.

To get started with the app, do the following:

1. Create a new project and name it WriteMore.

2. Add the following items from the User Interface palette: a TextBox, a Button, and a TinyWebDB.

3. Change the width of the text box to Fill Parent and the height to 70 pixels. This box will display the current story. Check the **MultiLine** property and uncheck the **Enabled** property. We want to handle multiple lines of text. We also don't want the user to type in here directly, so we'll disable it. Rename it to **CurrentStoryTextBox**.

4. Change the text of the button to read UPDATE. This button will be used to pull the current story from the online database. Rename the button to **UpdateStoryButton**.

5. Add another text box. This will be the one the player will use to add a word to the story. Set the width to Fill Parent and rename it as **NewWordTextBox**. If you want to be fancy, delete the text from it and change the hint property to read Word.

6. Add another button below the text box. Label this one Send! and rename it as **SendWordButton**.

7. To make it look nice and help your user, add some labels explaining the parts. You can use a horizontal arrangement for the label with the Update button, as in Figure 11.8.

Figure 11.8   The WriteMore app in the Designer. Use a horizontal arrangement to make the label and button appear at the top. The Title also can be changed as a property of Screen1.

8. Make sure your device is connected or your emulator is running. The app should look like Figure 11.9. Notice the hint in the word box!

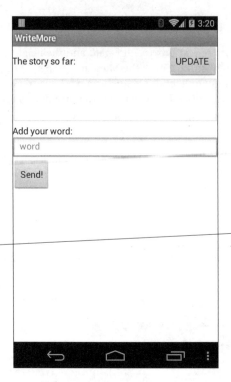

Figure 11.9   The WriteMore app running on a device. Notice the hint in the word box.

9. Now is the fun part! Switch over to the blocks view.

10. This app hinges on the TinyWebDB, which we will use often. To make things a little easier, set up your tag value as a variable. This way, whenever you need to use the tag with a TinyWebDB block, you can use a variable getter and know that the tag will be the same in all those instances. The tag text can be anything—make it unique by including your initials or name, to keep it from being overwritten in the database (see Figure 11.10). (You don't need to worry about that if you use a private TinyWebDB service.)

Figure 11.10   Making a variable for the DB tag. Also shown is the getter for the variable, which will be used whenever the tag is needed.

11. First comes the easiest part. Whenever the Update button is clicked, we want to send a request for the current story from the database, as in Figure 11.11.

Figure 11.11   Requesting the most recent story from the database.

12. The request we just made is only the request. After some short amount of time (probably too short for a human to notice), the response will arrive from the database and the **GotValue** event will run. We will use the **GotValue** event to update the screen (see Figure 11.12).

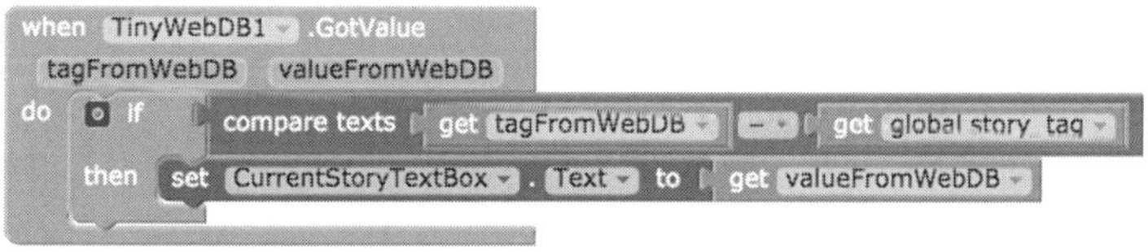

Figure 11.12   Updating the screen when the most recent story arrives from the database. The tag is also checked from the database to make sure it is the correct data.

13. One more feature is added to the **GotValue** block: an **if** block that checks to make sure the data we got back is the data associated with the correct tag. It is possible to ask for more than one tag; the only way to know which data is which is to check the tag that it comes back with (see Figure 11.12).

14. Usually, we would say "Try it out!" right now—and you should. But this won't really work yet because we don't have a way to put any data in the database yet. Reading data out won't be validated until we put data in, so let's do that!

15. The **SendWordButton** is the key to storing data. To play the game, we want to take the new word from the **NewWordTextBox** and add it to the end of the existing story, then resend that new story to the database. We'll use some pieces from the Text palette to do this (see Figure 11.13).

Figure 11.13   Sending a new word by adding the word to the existing story and then storing the whole thing.

16. *Now* you can try it! You might notice that sending the word works, but you don't *know* that it works unless you also press the Update button. TinyWebDB also provides an event named **ValueStored**, which fires after a value is stored in the database. We'll use that to automatically fetch the newest story (which also automatically updates the screen), as you can see in Figure 11.14.

Figure 11.14   After the new story is successfully stored, re-request the newest story to update the screen (and make sure it worked).

17. That's it! The app is done. For testing (and maybe for playing), you might want to add one more feature: the capability to reset the story in the database. Instead of adding a reset button, let's hide that feature. Each button has a **LongClick** event, which is a good way to sneak in extra functionality. We'll use the long press of the Update button to reset the story (see Figure 11.15).

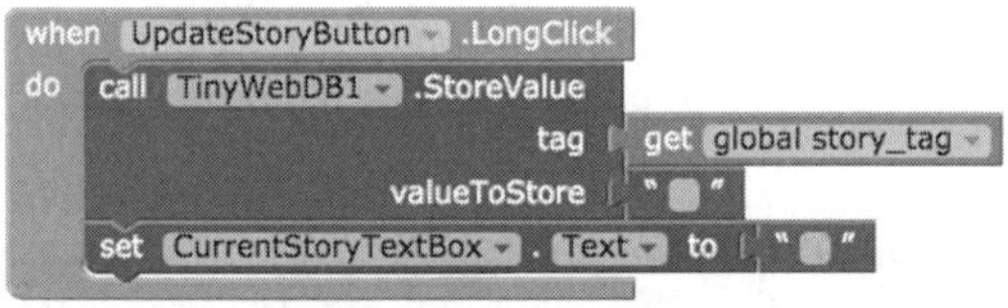

Figure 11.15   Hiding a reset feature in the Update button's **LongClick** event.

Additional Exercises

1. This app has one big possible bug: What happens when two players press Send! with different words at about the same time? (This is the same thing that happens if someone playing skips someone else's turn and plays early.)

2. Add some feedback to the user that lets the user know that the app is sending or updating. Be careful—you don't want to say that it's updating when it's not.

3. How else could you use this functionality? Perhaps you could program an app that allows users to add numbers as part of creating an equation. Think of other possible uses for a group activity app that uses database storage.

4. This functionality also could be useful in conducting a poll. Several users with the app could submit an answer to a poll question by using TinyDB. Think about how you could program this kind of an app, or consider whether a similar function would be desirable.

Summary

App Inventor provides an excellent method for learning how to store data with the TinyDB and TinyWebDB components. When you have data that can be saved on the device and that poses no security risks, go with TinyDB. It is useful in a lot of situations and can be set up quickly.

If your data needs to be shared online, go with the TinyWebDB option. This option enables data to be shared quickly and easily among users of your app. TinyWebDB was built specifically for App Inventor, but it is neither secure nor private. You can create your own TinyWebDB service, which reduces the chance of accidental deletion, but it is still inherently insecure storage and should not be used for any sensitive data or data that needs to exist for long periods of time.

FusionTables is a Google service that provides (relatively) easy access to a high-end, professional-grade database. FusionTables can store huge amounts of data, is easy to secure, and enables powerful queries to access the data you need. However, with that power comes complexity. FusionTables likely will take some time to fully set up, understand, and get working. Patience is key, but it's worth it.

Many web-based services have APIs, and App Inventor can use any API that is accessible over simple HTTP requests.

The introductory work you perform with databases in App Inventor can also be a springboard to doing higher-level work with other applications. After building the app in this chapter, consider how databases might enhance other applications that you build.

Distributing an App

One of the best rewards after all that hard work making an app is sharing it with others. Whether you are looking to just install your app on your own device, share it with friends, or submit it for worldwide distribution through Google Play, this chapter will have you ready to let others enjoy your work.

In this chapter, we discuss the following:

- Downloading the app from App Inventor as an APK file.
- Installing an APK file on your device.
- Creating an .aia file with your app, which is a preferable format for sharing it directly with others.
- Uploading the app to Google Play. This process also involves creating a developer account to make your app available for worldwide distribution.

Live Mode

To this point, your work has been in *Live Mode*, where you have been testing apps in real time while building them (see Figure 12.1). Live Mode, whether using the AI Companion app or the onscreen emulator, offers a good method for testing your app while building. Live Mode has its limitations, however. It can be used only while your device is connected to App Inventor.

In this chapter, we talk about how to build your app. Building transforms your app, which works in Live Mode, into a downloadable file that can be permanently installed on an Android device without needing to be connected to App Inventor. This file, which ends with .apk, is an Android application package file and is the same format used in the Play Store and any other Android app.

To get a more real-world example of how the app will perform on users' devices, you should download the entire app and test it on your own device first. Most of App Inventor works exactly the same when built for installation as it does in Live Mode, but because of a few subtle differences, you should always test. This is especially important if you use multiple screens. You want to test that the behavior is consistent from one screen size to another.

Figure 12.1   Live Mode is an excellent way to see your app develop. The emulator provides a real-time view while you are still programming it. The emulator and the Companion app both use Live Mode.

Security Settings

Before we proceed with installing an app on your device, you need to confirm a security setting in Android. By default, most Android devices don't allow users to install any apps that didn't come from the Google Play Store. This is to prevent users from installing apps from untrusted sources that could infect their device with malware. But here you are the source, and your friends will trust you, so they can feel good about installing your app. (Really, they can trust the app only as much as they trust you, but that's outside the scope of this book.)

Typically, this setting isn't an issue because the average Android user is just going to download and purchase apps through Google Play. Application developers and Android enthusiasts who want to experiment with new or untested apps load them directly to a device in a process known as *side loading*. This setting enables side loading.

Go to Settings on your device (see Figure 12.2). Then find the Security setting (see Figure 12.3).

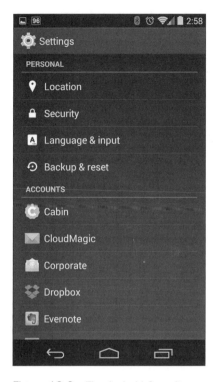

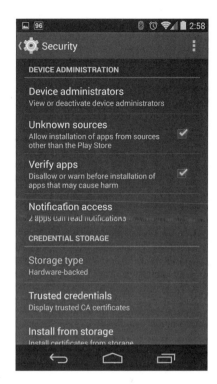

Figure 12.2   The Android Security settings are usually under a section labeled Personal (this varies depending on which Android device you are using).

Figure 12.3   Check the box labeled Unknown Sources.

Your device then will install the apps that we will be downloading from App Inventor. You will also be able to install apps from anywhere else in the world. Remember to install only apps that you trust, such as ones you created yourself.

Creating an APK File

As noted previously, the package file format for Android applications is the Android application package (APK). The actual file extension is simply .apk.

Two methods work for creating an APK file. First we look at how to download the file directly to your computer and provide options for moving it to your Android device. Then we examine using a QR code.

Downloading Directly to a Computer

To create an APK from your app, go to the Build menu (see Figure 12.4) and select App (Save .apk to My Computer).

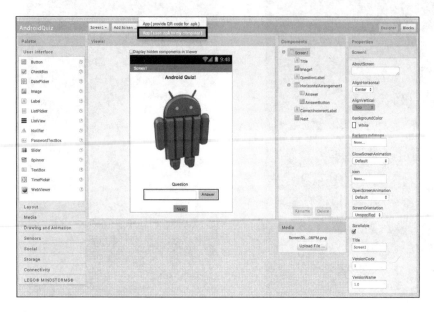

Figure 12.4   Select the option to download the APK directly to your computer.

> **Note**
>
> The build process usually takes less than 30 seconds, but it can take up to a few minutes if the build servers are busy. The build servers are different than the primary App Inventor web servers: there are a finite number of them, and they are shared among all App Inventor users.

App Inventor then downloads the file to your computer. Depending on your browser settings, either the file downloads to a preset location automatically (such as your Downloads folder) or you are asked where you want to save it (see Figure 12.5).

After a successful download, locate the file. The filename will end with the extension .apk (see Figure 12.6).

This file can then be moved to an Android device. You have multiple ways to do this; we cover the most straightforward options.

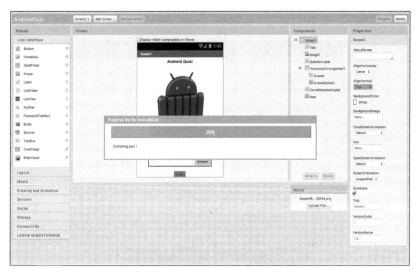

Figure 12.5 Downloading an APK to your computer. The file will be downloaded when the progress bar finishes.

AndroidQuiz.apk

Figure 12.6 An APK file downloaded from App Inventor, as seen in the file browser on the computer.

One good method is to connect your Android device to a computer and move the file. Connect the phone via USB to a computer and drag the file to the folder that represents the phone. Not all phones can do this, and you might need to choose an option on the phone's screen to enable file access.

Alternatively, you can upload the APK to a cloud service such as Google Drive or Dropbox and then open the file directly from your device (see Figure 12.7). Nearly every Android device supports this method, but it does involve signing in, sharing, and dealing with other account-management issues that come with cloud services.

You can also email the APK as an attachment and open it from the phone's email app.

Figure 12.7   Uploading the file to a service such as Google Drive is a fast and efficient method for getting it to your device.

Continuing with our Google Drive example, just a couple more steps are needed to get the APK up and working on your device.

Open the Drive app and locate the file (in this case, we have used AndroidQuiz, with the file named AndroidQuiz.apk—see Figure 12.8).

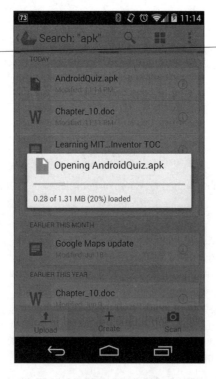

Figure 12.8   Find the app inside your cloud storage service (in this case, we are using Google Drive as an example).

After opening the file, you are taken to an installation screen (see Figure 12.9). Agree to the list of criteria and wait for the app to install on your device. These permissions reflect the specific hardware and software features the app needs to access on the phone or tablet. This changes depending on which components you include in your app. For example, the Location Sensor component requires permission to access the location-sensing hardware of the device. All App Inventor apps require a base set of permissions, including modifying the contents of storage (to store images and other files) and network access.

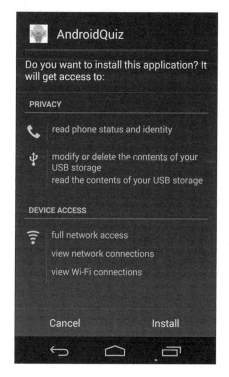

Figure 12.9   Click the Install button and get ready to start using the application.

The app then installs and is added to your application drawer (see Figure 12.10). Touch the app icon to open it, just as you would any other app on your device.

Now you can open the app. It should look and perform just as you programmed it (see Figure 12.11). The functionality will be similar to how it was used with the AI2 Companion app. However, it now is stored directly on your device, so you can try it at any time.

Figure 12.10   The AndroidQuiz app
has joined the other installed apps in
Android's application drawer.

Figure 12.11   Launch the app from the
application drawer, and it will run on your
device.

Downloading with a QR Code

Previously, we used a QR code to launch the AI2 Companion for testing the app. We use a
similar procedure here to create an APK file to be downloaded to your computer.

Return to the Build menu, this time selecting Build, App (Provide QR Code for .apk) as in
Figure 12.12.

After this step, you will see another progress bar indicating that the program is processing your
request. Then a QR code appears onscreen (see Figure 12.13).

The build process is exactly the same as with the download option, except that the file isn't
downloaded to your computer. The resulting APK file is stored on the App Inventor servers,
and the QR code contains the URL link to that file. That's all it is—a web link. This code and
link are valid for only a specific amount of time. Currently, this is two hours, and after that
time, the code will no longer work. That should be plenty of time to get your app downloaded
onto your phone.

Figure 12.12   Select App (Provide QR Code for .apk)

Figure 12.13   App Inventor creates a QR code, just as it did previously. In this case, scanning the code enables you to download the app to your Android device.

Use a general QR code reader to read the code—do not use the Companion app because it does not know how to read web links. If you don't have one built in, we recommend the ZXing barcode reader, which is available in the Play Store.

Launch the code reader (*not* the Companion app) on your device. Press the Scan QR code button and hold the device close enough to the computer screen for the app to scan the code (see Figure 12.14).

Figure 12.14   Use a general code scanner, like ZXing, to read the barcode App Inventor generates. The barcode will remain active for two hours.

Select Open after the reader extracts the link from the code. You then are taken to the browser, which downloads your file. Most likely, you will need to select the file from the notification drawer at the top of the Android screen. If you missed it, you can always find it in the Downloads folder. When you open the file, you will see the same installation screen observed during the download walkthrough. Again, after you agree to the installation, the app installs on your device and is added to the application drawer.

Either method is effective in getting the app to your device. It all comes down to personal preferences and workflow to determine the preferred course of action.

Creating an .aia File

Another option for downloading your app is to create an **.aia** file, which is generally used when distributing the project source to others for collaboration.

This enables someone else to upload your app into his or her own App Inventor account and then make additional adjustments.

Alternatively, someone else could remix the app by making improvements or other adjustments to your original concept. This method also is useful if you are collaborating with others, as a way to problem-solve or provide examples of how to create a particular feature. As you build more complex apps, you might find more opportunities to work with others and share ideas about what types of strategies work best with App Inventor.

To download your app as an .aia file, go to the My Projects menu and then select an app for distribution. After selecting the check box, click Project and select Export Selected Project (.aia) to My Computer (see Figure 12.15).

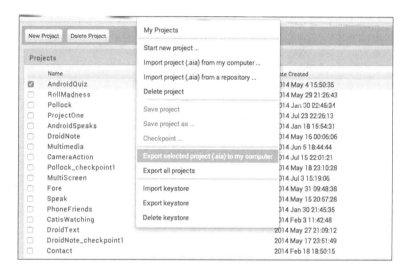

Figure 12.15   Export the selected project (.aia) to your computer. The file then downloads and is available for distribution to others.

Importing an app is also a fairly straightforward procedure. From the same menu, select Import Project (.aia) from My Computer. You can then upload the file, and it will be added to your database of projects (see Figure 12.16).

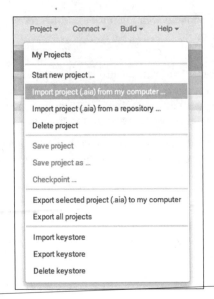

Figure 12.16   Importing an .aia file is done through the Project menu.

Exercise: App Distribution

The previous method of downloading and sharing an app is useful for trying it out on your own device or sharing it with others.

However, your ambitions might be greater than that. If your app is of high enough quality or you are looking to gain experience, it could be time to upload your app to the Google Play Store. This is the primary app storefront for Android apps, making it accessible to virtually any Android device worldwide.

Version Codes

Apps that are published to Google Play require a **VersionCode** and **VersionName**. These are managed in the Designer, inside the Properties panel of the **Screen1** component (see Figure 12.17). Google Play and the Android system use these codes to know when apps need to be updated.

The **VersionCode** is the number that really matters for update tracking. It must always be a whole number, and each new version of the app (which you submit) must have a greater value than the previous version. The user never sees this number, but the user's phone updates if the new file has a higher **VersionCode** than the one already installed.

Figure 12.17   The **VersionCode** and **VersionName** are found in the Properties box of Screen1.

The **VersionName** is visible to the user, both in Google Play and in the Android device's settings. You can write whatever you want here, including letters, numbers, and many special characters. You can use this code to make or match whatever versioning scheme you like.

Say you have a version of your app on the Play Store; it is **VersionCode** 1, and the **VersionName** is 1.0. You then make a small change and want to push an update. For an update to replace the previous version, you must bump up the **VersionCode**, so you change it to 2. You then change the **VersionName** to 1.1, which better describes to your users that the change was small.

Other valid examples of **VersionName** include the date (2014-08-18v1), maybe a code word (tango), or just a version name with your own flair, such as r1 instead of v1 (read as "revision one" instead of "version one").

Android and the Play Store don't care what you put in **VersionName**, as long as the **VersionCode** number is consistent and increasing.

Google Play Developer Console

The Google Play Developer Console is your main hub for uploading apps to Google Play (see Figure 12.18).

To begin, open a new browser tab and enter **play.google.com/apps/publish** into the address. Make sure you are signed in with your Google account.

Figure 12.18   The Google Play Developer Console.

The Developer Console requires a developer account, which you have to sign up for separately from your Google account. Once in the Developer Console, if you don't have a developer account, you will probably go directly to the signup page (see Figure 12.19). If you can't find it, the address is https://play.google.com/apps/publish/signup/.

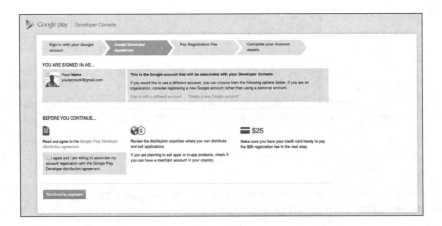

Figure 12.19   The signup page for the Developer Console.

Creating a developer account costs $25, and you must agree to the Google Play Developer distribution agreement.

When you have a developer account, you can upload an app. To prepare, build your App Inventor project and download the APK file. You need to have the APK downloaded to your computer so that you can upload it into the Developer Console.

Let's get started. With your APK file ready to go, make sure you are on the All Applications screen of the Developer Console; click the large teal button that reads Add New Application (see Figure 12.20).

ALL APPLICATIONS
+ Add new application

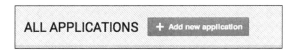

Figure 12.20 The button to add a new app in Google Play.

The Add New Application pop-up screen appears. It asks you to enter the default language for the app and give it a title (see Figure 12.21).

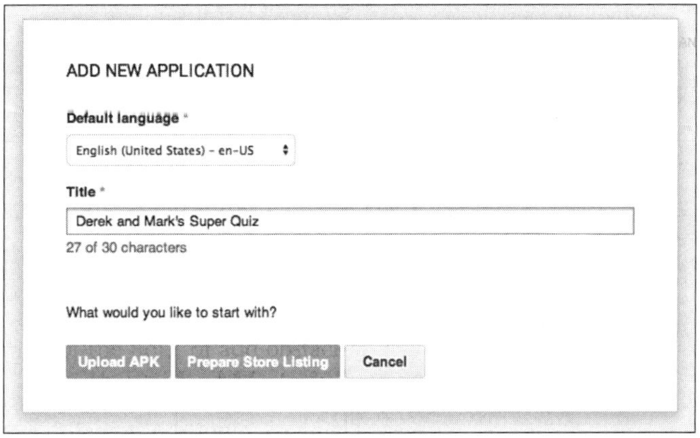
ADD NEW APPLICATION
Default language *
English (United States) – en-US
Title *
Derek and Mark's Super Quiz
27 of 30 characters
What would you like to start with?
Upload APK
Prepare Store Listing
Cancel

Figure 12.21 The Add New Application pop-up, where you name your app.

From there, you can choose whether you'd like to first upload an APK or prepare the store listing. Both need to be done, and you can do them in either order. The store listing is where you put the information that people will read when they find your app in the store. The APK is just that—the package file that Google Play will distribute for you.

Prepare Store Listing

The store listing is where you fill in all the details about your app, from text descriptions to pictures showing your app at work. To publish your app, you *must* have at least two images to upload with it: the high-res icon and a featured graphic. The Store Listing page is long and detailed, and it explains every part that you need to provide. Items with a green asterisk (*) are mandatory, and the app listing will not be created or updated without all those items.

Be prepared: The Store Listing is very specific about description lengths and image formats. For example, the Hi-res icon must be 512x512 pixels and must be saved as a 32-bit PNG image. The featured graphic, which appears as a banner at the top of your app's listing page, must be 1024x500 pixels, but it can be a JPG or a PNG type.

Filling out the Store Listing takes time and patience. You can save your progress, allowing you to leave and return to it, but you cannot publish updates until you provide all the mandatory parts.

Upload APK

When you upload an APK, you can put it into one of three levels of publication: Alpha Testing, Beta Testing, or Production (see Figure 12.22). These levels have successively larger audiences, and anyone outside that specific audience will not see the app. You can set up a small group of people to be Alpha testers, which is usually limited to you and the development team. The Beta level is intended for a larger, but still restricted, group of test users. Only in Production will the app be publicly visible to the whole world.

When you have an app in Production, if you want to make an update, you can upload another APK file and put it into the Alpha or Beta levels. Your test users in those groups will see the update, but the public will be completely unaware of the new version until you push it into Production.

If you don't have test users, a team, or anyone you want to see your app before it becomes public, you can push the APK straight into Production, and it will become publicly available.

Figure 12.22   The three levels of APK publication.

Application Keys

Whenever you build a project, that APK file is signed with a key file that is unique to your App Inventor account. For most uses, you don't have to worry about this. When dealing with Google Play, however, the key becomes very important: *An app in Google Play can be updated only with APKs that have the same key signature as the original APK that was uploaded.*

When you upload an APK, the key that signed that particular file becomes permanently linked to that app in Google Play. If you ever want to upload a newer APK, it must also be signed with the same key. If you lose that key, or lose access to the App Inventor account that holds the key, you will never be able to update the app in Google Play again. Many apps, even professional ones, have been abandoned because of issues with keys.

To help you, App Inventor has provided a way to download, upload, and delete the keystore that is stored in your App Inventor account. You can find these features under the Project menu.

When you first build an app to be uploaded to Google Play, it is a good idea to also export the App Inventor keystore and save that somewhere on your computer. It is also a good idea to export the .aia file and also save it. With both the .aia project file and the keystore, you will be able to re-create your development environment, even in a different App Inventor account.

> **Warning**
>
> *If you lose the key, or you lose the App Inventor account that holds the key, you will not be able to update the app in Google Play.* This is one of the few places where you cannot undo a mistake.

Update Time

Any changes that you make to the Developer Console take a few hours to become visible to the users of the world. Google Play takes time to propagate your changes throughout its network. Users often will not see an updated app download for 6 to 12 hours. Updates to the Store Listing could be visible in 3 hours. In general, make sure you leave an extra day in your production schedule between your update and the time you need that update to be visible.

For example, an APK that is pushed into Production from Beta Testing minutes before a launch party will probably not yet be available, making the launch party rather anticlimactic.

Summary

App Inventor offers many different opportunities for sharing your app: You can download it to your own device, share it with others, or upload it to Google Play.

If you have done the latter, you are no longer seeking to be an Android developer—you *are* one. Even if your app is relatively simple, it marks an important milestone in the process to building apps for the Android platform.

The journey through MIT App Inventor should have taught you valuable skills for computational thinking and application design. With this skill set in place, you can take this knowledge as far as you wish and build apps of deeper sophistication and complexity.

Index

informIT.com
THE TRUSTED TECHNOLOGY LEARNING SOURCE

PEARSON InformIT is a brand of Pearson and the online presence for the world's leading technology publishers. It's your source for reliable and qualified content and knowledge, providing access to the leading brands, authors, and contributors from the tech community.

Addison-Wesley · Cisco Press · IBM Press · Microsoft Press

PEARSON IT CERTIFICATION · PRENTICE HALL · Que · SAMS · vmware PRESS

LearnIT at InformIT

Looking for a book, eBook, or training video on a new technology? Seeking timely and relevant information and tutorials. Looking for expert opinions, advice, and tips? **InformIT has a solution**.

- Learn about new releases and special promotions by subscribing to a wide variety of monthly newsletters. Visit **informit.com/newsletters**.

- FREE Podcasts from experts at **informit.com/podcasts**.

- Read the latest author articles and sample chapters at **informit.com/articles**.

- Access thousands of books and videos in the Safari Books Online digital library. **safari.informit.com**.

- Get Advice and tips from expert blogs at **informit.com/blogs**.

Visit **informit.com** to find out all the ways you can access the hottest technology content.

Are you part of the IT crowd?

Connect with Pearson authors and editors via RSS feeds, Facebook, Twitter, YouTube and more! Visit **informit.com/socialconnect**.

ALWAYS LEARNING · **PEARSON**